The Ma[ ]
Champi[ ]
How Children
Become Sporting
Greats

By Edward Lowe

First Printing, 2018

ISBN 9781729022054

For all enquiries, email edwardlowe13@gmail.com

To Mum and Dad,
For passing on the sport obsession

Contents

Prologue

Usain Bolt takes off his warm-up top and begins to bounce on his toes behind his blocks, unable to stand still in a moment like this.[1] The camera pans to the man for whom so much is hoped. The 2007 World Champion, Bolt is the favourite to win Olympic gold in Beijing, but the question is whether he can deliver on the biggest stage of all. The camera moves along the line of competitors as they are introduced to the crowd, those in the Birds Nest roaring their appreciation as it settles on Bolt. He is undoubtedly their favourite. TVs around the world show a grinning face without a care in the world as he plays serious for a second before returning to that infectious smile. Bolt has already breathed life into a sport that was desperate for a hero following years of crippling doping allegations.

The Bolt pose, soon to take over the world, is struck by the man everyone hopes will succeed. He points down the track towards the finish line that could change his life. Richard Thompson of Trinidad and Tobago is introduced next. Along with Bolt's compatriot Asafa Powell, these two are considered Bolt's biggest rivals, with many tipping Powell to fulfil his potential and finally win a global title.

The crowd hushes as the sprinters take their places. Usain settles in the blocks, hands delicately placed on the brand-new track. In position, head lowered, his body cuts a different shape to the rest of the sprinters; his angular shoulder blades pointing to the sky in stark contrast to the round, muscular shoulders of Powell and the rest. The sprinters are like highly coiled springs, ready to explode off the start line. A hundred metres stands between them and the gold medal they had strained for over the course of four years. This race stands between them and glory.

The shout of 'Set!' comes from the starter. All is still; you could hear a pin drop inside the stadium. Then the gun goes, and the roar of over 90,000 spectators assaults the track. Bolt bursts out of the blocks, a little behind the pack as his long levers strive to accelerate. His feet splay wide in his lane, the golden boots moving with feverish energy. Thompson makes a fast start and is metres ahead of Bolt, running with the confidence of a man who thinks he can win. Powell emerges from the line of competitors as a leader too.

Suddenly, it is almost like Bolt is being catapulted forward by an unknown force. For the mere mortals around him, acceleration slows, but Bolt continues, legs churning ever quicker as he approaches halfway. His powerful strides differ from the dynamically efficient running of the competitors, as if he is a tearaway child running with the freedom of youth. All eyes are on him as he is one metre in front, and then in the blink of an eye he is out on his own. There is no chance of anyone catching him.

As he stretches his lead further and further ahead, it's

hard to comprehend how there can be such a disparity between him and a field which features the world's fastest-ever sprinters. Jaws are dropping even before Bolt produces an act of pure showmanship that will never be repeated.

At 80 metres, he knows he has won the race. With the other seven competitors in a line striving for the minor medals, there is Bolt, arms spread wide in celebration, legs still churning those long, elegant strides. He beats his chest, turning to the crowd to his right, a raw scream leaving his mouth as he powers over the line.

The audaciousness of those celebrations during the race is unlike anything anyone has ever seen in an Olympic final. He crosses the line all on his own. Take-your-breath-away showmanship is only matched by what flashes onto the scoreboard: a finishing time of 9.69 seconds. A world-record time that few thought was even humanly possible. Imagine if he had sprinted the whole way?

Not content with finishing the 100 metres, he barely slows down as he wheels round the track, celebrating with his fans as everyone realises the special moment in sporting history they have just witnessed. He poses; he dances and he laughs, unable to contain the joy of winning a gold medal. It's Bolt's first step on the path to immortality.

***

Nadia Comăneci turns abruptly to face the Uneven Bars at the Montreal Olympics in 1976. [2] Her announcement is met by polite applause from the crowd. Comăneci's coach, Béla Károlyi, offers a final piece of advice to her, whispering an instruction. In her white leotard with stripes of yellow, red and blue, the 14-year-old has a look of total calm across her face that belies her age and the stage she is on. Instead, her eyes show a steely competitive edge.

A lot of pressure is on the shoulders of the young Romanian. Not only was she looking to win for herself, but huge expectations had been placed on her coach and her team to bring glory to her nation of Romania. The entire country was watching and hoping for success with bated breath.

Comăneci adjusts her position on the floor a little, rubbing her chalked hands together and taking one last deep breath as she mentally prepares for the effort she is about to undertake. She slowly rises onto the balls of her feet, and then the change of pace comes. She runs with effortless fluency, launching off the board and vaulting over the lower bar to reach the higher bar beyond, grasping it tightly as she swings herself into a roll and then a handstand.

As she holds herself expertly above the higher bar, she begins the routine, flowing into a reverse catch. The pace fluctuates between fast bursts of controlled aggression and fluency, punctuated by beautifully held positions above the bars. It is a display of routinised perfection. Her moves are not just perfection of what already exists, but also push the boundary of what is possible as a gymnast, combining for the first time grace with a powerful physicality.

After a flurry of complex moves, she gathers momentum as she begins her finish. She completes a handless somersault around the lower bar using only her hips. The bar slings her like a shot, and she seems to fly on her finishing move; arms spread wide and back arched, looking more bird than woman.

Take a freeze frame of that moment, and the height at which she is flying is breathtaking. With perfect arched back and arms outstretched, she moves from horizontal to vertical. She lands with a small hop and salutes the crowd with the air of someone who could do this in her sleep. She quickly moves off the apparatus, preparing for the next event.

The scores come in; the board shows a 1.00. Coach Károlyi, always there to defend his gymnasts, is ready to lynch the judges. It is quickly explained that the scoreboard actually only goes up to 9.99 – they never thought they would see a 10 in the competition.

Nadia had been given the first perfect 10 in Olympic history. The crowd erupts, and Comăneci returns for another small salute to the crowd, this time breaking into a smile. The Romanian changed the gymnastics world forever, and became the inspiration for young girls across the world.

***

With an air of confidence, Michael Phelps enters the Aquatics Centre in Beijing that has become like a second home to him over the past week.[3] He is dressed in a large, white warm-up jacket, the US flag displayed prominently on the chest. While others are quickly stripping down to their swimsuits, Phelps goes slowly and deliberately through his warm-up routine, one earphone in. His concentration and coolness are almost chilling. Finally, he takes off his warm-up gear, getting down to his swimsuit. During the name announcements over the tannoy, Phelps' demeanour changes as he enters 'the zone'. He shakes those freakishly long arms, slowly bending his neck left and right, goggles now covering his eyes. While others look pumped up and excited, Phelps looks focused, retaining his edge despite the potential enormity of this moment.

Phelps had already won six golds at the 2008 Olympics, and with two races to go, the supposed unreachable record of Mark Spitz's seven golds in a single Games seemed within his grasp. Out of the final two events, the major challenge was the 100m Butterfly he was about to compete in. Tired after so many swims, this shorter sprint event needed perfect execution for him to win.

Cavic, Crocker and Le Clos are all drawn in lanes around him. They are serious threats over this shorter distance: Crocker holds the world record, Cavic has unmatched acceleration, while Le Clos is an exceptional talent. Introductions complete, all the athletes step on to the blocks. As the rest crouch, ready for the starter's orders, Phelps wraps his long arms around himself one more time, slapping his body. A final piece of intimidation. The sound echoes around the arena.

'Take your marks—', the swimmers tense – Beep! The race begins, the swimmers diving into the pool with a small splash, before pushing through the water with urgency. Cavic goes out fast, knowing he is going to have to build a lead to have a chance of holding off Phelps in the later stages. Almost immediately, Phelps is a stroke down on his rival, driving to make sure he keeps up with the pack and doesn't get stuck in Cavic's wake.

At the halfway touch, the swimmers form an almost perfect arrow shape – except for Phelps. He lags behind leader Cavic in the lane to his left and has US compatriot Crocker ahead of him on his right too. The commentators shout, panic in their voices, as they realise that Phelps is in trouble.

The swim for home begins, but the pattern of the race begins to change. A couple of strokes in and the black cap of Phelps is beginning to eat into the lead held by his competitors. Phelps overhauls Crocker and Le Clos, but Cavic tantalisingly holds on to his lead. With 20 metres to go, Cavic still leads, pushing hard as he strains to maintain his advantage. Phelps' progress has slowed. His monstrous strokes have a desperate look now. The reeling in of Cavic is continuing, but the finish seems too close, the distance to make up too great.

Again and again, Phelps' strokes only reduce the distance to Cavic by a little; he's gaining on Cavic, but painfully slowly. With 10 metres to go, Phelps is still making inroads. Five metres to go, and it seems that all is lost; Cavic will hang on for victory and prevent the fairy tale ending. Two metres to go, the race belongs to Cavic. One metre to go, Cavic takes one more stroke and pushes his fingertips out for the touch. Phelps, too far from the wall for a full stroke, whips his arms through in a half stroke.

It seems to the crowd that Cavic has hung on, and there is a deflated atmosphere that the record has escaped Phelps. Phelps turns around to face the giant screen and see the results. He opens his mouth wide. To his, and everyone else's surprise, he has triumphed by 0.01 of a second. The explosion of joy is incredible. Phelps touched second but pushed harder against the plate and registered the fastest time. There could not have been a tighter finish.

The shock across Phelps' face is real. It dawns on him that he has just completed something that many thought was impossible. He points to his family before slamming the water, letting out a scream of relief as much as joy. The muscles ripple as every sinew of his being seems to be charged with adrenaline. He had done it; by some miracle, he had matched Spitz's record. The magic eight golds in a single Games was going to happen.

***

Muhammad Ali walks out into the sweltering, fever-pitch atmosphere of the 20th May Stadium, Kinshasa, Zaire, to chants of 'Ali, boumaye!' (Ali, kill him!). [4] He jumps into the ring and prowls around it, a look in his eyes that is hard to pin down: Fear? Focus? Determination? All are equally likely. As he takes off his gown, his skin already has a thin film of sweat across it. Ali's white shorts with black trim are a symbolic contrast to Foreman's red shorts with yellow trim[5] – calm against fire.

During the introductions, George Foreman is all power and silent aggression, staring down Ali and looking like he genuinely wants to kill him. Ali is wound up, shouting at Foreman, continuing to talk the game that had captured the world's imagination in the months leading up to the fight. Foreman has been put through a lot in the build-up, and the genuine animosity is palpable. This had gone beyond publicity.

The bell rings for the first round, and Muhammad Ali begins to dance like everyone knew he would. He pops his punches, aggressive and on the attack, catching Foreman with surprise as he produces a right- rather than left-hand jab time and time again. Foreman launches a few thunderous strikes to Ali's body, warning him. But unlike many before him, Ali takes these blows and sucks it up. He comes back at Foreman, firing more quickfire shots in his direction. It's an intriguing first round, pace against power, one not characterised by the usual wariness of heavyweight boxing.

As the second round begins, the style of the fight changes entirely. Ali hangs back and defends, pressed against the ropes, taking blow after blow from Foreman. He looks weak, unable to sustain his early pace in the face of such thunderous strikes from Foreman. Sensing blood, Foreman jumps on the opportunity to finish his man and finally shut Ali up. He pulverises him, striking his head repeatedly with pure brutality.

Ali survives the round, but it seems only a matter of time before he is finished. The third round follows a similar pattern of total dominance, as Ali continues to attempt to deflect and avoid punches, and Foreman continues his relentless march forward. Ali is now backed up into a corner, but manages to throw enough back with interest at the end of the round to draw wild shouts from the crowd, baying for Ali to attack and put Foreman on the back foot.

In the middle of this battle, Ali talks to Foreman. He tells him his punches are nothing, that he could take this all day, that this was not the great George Foreman he had been told about. He goads Foreman while they hold, whispering in his ear. Foreman hits even harder in response, the red mist descending even further.

As the rounds go on, the pace slows, but the pattern remains the same. Ali hangs off the ropes, looking for all the world as if he is about to fall. Foreman, almost like in a practice fight, unleashes huge left hooks at will which make the audience wince. Most are deflected, but some reach their sweet spot. Ali takes it all, aiming to simply stay in the fight.

As the fight continues, Foreman becomes more desperate. No one has ever received so much punishment from him and remained standing. He swings harder to get his opponent out of the ring. He takes big long arching shots, many missing by a distance. Head down, body slumped, Foreman had lost the power and accuracy that he started with. Ali sways, struggling to concentrate after the constant battering, mind fuzzed by the memory-loss inducing hits from the hardest puncher in history. The pair look like drunks outside a bar after closing, grappling and swinging sporadically.

The eighth round starts, and Ali does not immediately go to the ropes. He cracks a few shots to the head of an unexpecting Foreman, knocking it back. Foreman bounces on his feet in response, trying to breathe life into his exhausted body. He launches one huge left hand that almost throws his own body out of the arena. Ali continues to whisper in Foreman's ear, telling him to keep punching.

Ali lands a right-hand square to the jaw. He senses a weakness and his eyes widen. This is the moment! He strikes again at his opponent, and Foreman wobbles. Ali realises that he is there for the taking. He bounds towards the middle of the ring, and hits Foreman with a left and a right. Foreman tries to respond but he has nothing left to give. Ali continues to pummel him, showing speed he had not displayed since the first round.

One more right hand from Ali, and Foreman is falling. It almost happens in slow motion, as he staggers to keep his feet, knowing he will not be able to get up again. His arms flailing in desperation, his body thumps the canvas, completely spent. The roar from the crowd is deafening. The Champ has won.

Ali only has enough energy left to salute the crowd as his team jump into the ring. He has done the impossible and defeated the most feared fighter the world has ever seen. He seems overcome with relief that it is over. In a glittering career, nothing Ali achieved would top the Rumble in the Jungle.

***

The audacious celebration of Usain Bolt 20 metres from the finish, the total perfection of Nadia Comăneci's Uneven Bars, the impossible comeback of Michael Phelps, the breath-taking Rumble in the Jungle win for Muhammad Ali; these iconic sporting moments are such incredible feats that it seems impossible that they could be achieved by mere mortals. They are moments that transcend their individual sport.

What further defies comprehension is that these performances are completed in the biggest competitions of these athletes' lives. Whereas most of us would be quivering in our boots if the success of our entire career depended on a single race or event, the greatest sporting champions produce their best-ever performances. The puzzle of how these athletes can produce these performances is something we will attempt to untangle in this book.

All these athletes, at the most basic level, started from the same place as us. What factors transformed the world's greatest champions from children into the Goliaths with unprecedented success in their sport?

Malcolm Gladwell's *Outliers: The Story of Success* [6] argued that, contrary to popular belief, natural talent isn't the dominant factor in success. The attention his theory garnered stemmed primarily from highlighting Anders Ericsson's study[7] and Gladwell suggesting that it required 10,000 hours of practice to become an expert in any field. The practice argument jarred with many people's view of success and sparked the imagination of what anyone could achieve with the right environment and dedication. We have seen a subsequent countermovement purporting the importance of genetics, explaining how genes can influence our outcomes in extremely complex ways. David Epstein looks at why those who train the same amount can have vastly different results, despite the same practice environment.[8] His findings point towards genes being dominant; not just in defining physical traits, but also mental ones which are important for success in athletes. Generally, there has been a mellowing from both sides of the argument to agree that both practice and genetic factors matter.

This book takes a different approach to trying to answer this question. Delving into the autobiographical and biographical accounts of the childhoods of the world's greatest athletes and combining it with studies from the fields of psychology, sport and child development, we can understand how sporting champions became the best, and the factors that contributed to their successes.

Although much has been written about sporting success, there has never been a systematic review of the childhoods of the world's very best athletes. These are gold-standard case studies when considering sporting development. By looking at the greatest athletes of all time during the years when they developed quickest, we can evaluate the existing theories and learn crucial additional lessons about sporting development.

This book finds that there is a common mentality amongst all of the sporting champions that is developed in childhood and separates our champions from the rest. The mindset starts with a burning competitiveness that is at the centre of everything they do and provides the primary sporting motivation throughout their lives. This attribute is combined with a longer-term motivation: a combination of a deep passion for the sport and a desire for fame and glory. These longer-term motivations vary in terms of importance throughout their childhoods, often with fame becoming more important as passion fades due to intensive training.

In childhood, these athletes have a hatred of failure, but also a hatred of quitting; despite not enjoying losing, these kids did whatever it took to become the best rather than trying something else. Doing whatever it takes is meant in its most literal sense here; the level of sacrifice and commitment is awe-inspiring.

This led to the mindset that distinguished these kids from their peers, even at a young age. This is despite our future champions often grappling with significant disadvantages in childhood, ranging from medical conditions to family difficulties.

This mentality is forged by the environmental around them; with everything from sporting institutions to parents playing their part in shaping the minds of youngsters in their path towards success. We will look specifically at what, in the case of each of our champions, was the main factor that helped develop their mindset.

This mindset will be referred to as the 'Champion Mindset'. Bolt, Phelps, Comăneci and Ali developed this mindset during their childhood. It was in their career-defining moments, with the whole world watching, that we got to see it come to the forefront. They are fundamentally different in the way they think to the rest of us.

The Champion Mindset leads to the behaviours that many often seek to understand in children who are successful in sport; the huge number of practice hours they dedicate to their sport, and their ability to perform in high pressure scenarios. Practice in childhood, both in terms of quantity and quality, is the result of the Champion Mindset rather than being the root cause for success. Without the thought process behind it, the practice is ineffectual.

Of course, the world is much more complicated than this simple equation of cause and effect. In childhood, a lack of control over life can mean a multitude of different ways in which obstacles could block the path to success. Genetics can play an important role, particularly in terms of determining physical attributes in specific sports where they are important. There is also the importance of luck – the random events that happen in our life that can determine so much. The best that can be done is to provide the best opportunity for success. There will always be an element of randomness. But to be successful, the complex mentality of champions is a prerequisite.

We will explore all of these ideas in more detail within this book. From how the Williams sisters changed the game of tennis in Compton to how Sachin Tendulkar mastered batting in the cricket melting pot of Mumbai, each case brings a unique flavour to our understanding of what was important in childhood to our champions' success. They could not be more diverse, but the accounts of each one of the champions are incredible. The sheer dedication, focus and energy put into their sport and the obstacles they had to overcome is beyond what most of us could imagine. I hope you will share my admiration for these special few.

By better understanding these sporting champions, we can learn how to effectively develop the sporting champions of the future too. By looking at the stories of how the world's greatest athletes grew up, we can understand the mindset to encourage, the environment that should be created, the practice techniques to be implemented and the potential costs to pursuing success in elite sport, particularly during childhood. Looking at the specifics of the journeys of these champions will reveal many practical lessons for coaches and parents to implement for their children, as well as highlighting some of the potential obstacles.

By analysing this topic, this book will also help to answer that nagging question that many an amateur adult athlete asks themselves:

Could I have made it to the top?

1

Competitiveness

Michael Jordan has always been a great physical specimen, but he is distinctly average in the context of the NBA. His listed height is 6 ft. 6 in. tall,[1] an inch shorter than the average NBA player.[2] He has a listed weight of 216 pounds,[3] about 6 pounds lighter than the average player.[4] He had great speed, but nothing exceptional compared to his competitors. Yet, he became the greatest basketball player of all time.

While at high school, his athleticism was something that teammates, journalists and opposition coaches alike marvelled at. But ask those who spent every day with him, and it was a mental rather than a physical trait that stood out most on the court. Jordan's competitiveness defined him.

Biographer Ronald Lazenby describes Jordan's all-consuming desire to win:

> At each step along his path, others would express amazement at how hard he competed. At every level, he was driven by

something that others couldn't see. On the basketball court it was as if everything that he was had been wound into a fury. Combined with his evolving physical gifts, this fury became a spectacle that the many witnesses along the way say they will never forget.[5]

The roots of Jordan's hardwired competitiveness began in his early years growing up in Wilmington, North Carolina. After moving a number of times while Michael was an infant, the family of seven settled in a large, split-level brick and clapboard house that Michael's father, James, had built on a 12-acre plot of land. It was here that he would call home right up until his university days.

Michael's two older brothers would often tinker with cars alongside their father, who was a keen motorhead. It was only due to his engineering ingenuity that the family had a car at all. Mainly through disinterest, Michael didn't know anything about fixing cars, a fact that irritated his father greatly. He didn't hide it from his youngest son. When Michael occasionally tried to help, he was met with the stinging retort:

'Just go on in the house with the women'.[6]

No other words spoken to Michael during his childhood would sear into his brain quite like those from his father. His ineptitude with a spanner was humiliating to his father and made Michael ashamed of himself. It was his father's affront to his manhood that began to stoke the burning fire of competitiveness in Jordan very early in his childhood, creating a desire to prove his dad wrong and show what he was capable of. After his career in the NBA had taken off, Michael would confess to his sister that his father's declaration of his worthlessness became a driving force that motivated him throughout his career.

Apart from cars, James Jordan's second love was for baseball. As a result, from when Michael was old enough to hold a mitt, he was learning the game. Given Michael showed potential, his father decided to put up a hoop in their front yard so that older brother Larry would have an alternative sport to play. He figured that Michael would play baseball and Larry would take up basketball.

But the minute the hoop was fixed in the front yard, basketball started to become a fascination for Michael, as well as his older brother. One-on-one became a daily fixture between the two. Eleven-year-old Michael had the height advantage over his brother, but he was built like a beanpole. Larry would use his stronger physicality to bully Michael around the court.

The contests were far from playful. They would trash talk each other, and the contests would quickly become physical. When the yelling became too much, their mother would order them inside the house to calm down. Every single night, the two brothers would be out there competing against each other.

For the first 18 months, Larry beat Michael relentlessly. He took great pleasure in doing so, and never took it easy on his little brother. But despite this constant battering at the hands of his sibling, Michael would keep coming back for more, slowly learning to use his height advantage to better Larry. In the end, they became so evenly matched that they were like a mirror of each other.

Competition between Larry and Michael Jordan was not restricted to basketball. They wanted to beat each other at everything. Michael remembers how competition affected everything in their lives: 'We had this barbecue pit that we'd use as the backstop and we'd play baseball with a tennis ball. If I lost, I had to keep playing until I won. That's why, more often than not, it would end in a fight.'[7]

Michael was already dreaming of basketball success. "'I remember Michael walking into the kitchen [at age 9]", his mother, Deloris, recalls, "and saying that Russia had won [the gold medal in basketball over Doug Collins' U.S. team in Munich, the ensuing dispute over a last-second ruling one of the most controversial in Olympic history]". He said, "I'm going to be in the Olympics one day and I'm going to make sure we win." I smiled to myself and said, "Honey, that takes a lot to win the gold medal". But he never lost that dream.'

Once he entered Laney High School, Jordan became even more infatuated with basketball. He was particularly keen to shoot hoops if he had someone to compete with. In the preseason before his junior year, his nemesis was Harvest Leroy Smith.

Already 6 ft. 6 in. tall, Leroy towered over the 5 ft. 9 in. Michael. Michael's quickness against Leroy's height led to tough competition as both looked to play to their strengths. Harvest Leroy Smith remembers that preseason well:

> He and I practised every day together and he always had to win. If it was a game of Horse and you beat him, you would have to go and play another game until he won.[8]

Infamously, despite all of this preseason training, Michael didn't make the Varsity High School team as a junior and was instead selected to play for the Junior Varsity (JV) team. Jordan was deeply hurt and wanted to quit the game. It was only at the insistence of his mother that he kept playing. But once training began back at Laney, Jordan was again bitten by the bug. He continued to improve and his competitiveness led him to take more of a leadership role on the JV team.

His coach that year, Fred Lynch, explains that not selecting Jordan for the Varsity team was a conscious decision for his development: 'We thought he'd be better off playing on the JV team. He didn't sulk; he worked. We knew Michael was good, but we wanted him to play more.'

His leading role in the JV began to impress the head coaches at the high school. Head Coach Pop Herring took a particular interest him and went above and beyond to help him improve. Pop would pick up Michael from his home and take him to school early so that they could work on his basketball before lessons started. Instead of sitting on the bench as part of the Varsity team, Jordan spent his junior year with an increasingly leading role in the JV side and getting plenty of practice time with the head coach. What shone through as much as his ability at that age was how badly he wanted to win – not just games, but every quarter, minute and second.

Ron Coley, one of those supporting the coaching of the Varsity team, saw Jordan compete as he entered the gym for a Varsity game:

> There were nine kids on the court just coasting, but there was one kid playing his heart out. The way he was playing I thought his team was down one point with two minutes to play. So I looked up at the clock and his team was down 20 points and there was only one minute to play. It was Michael, and I quickly learned he was always like

that.[9]

Michael's competitiveness would extend to all aspects of his life. As it became increasingly clear that basketball was his best potential route to success, younger sister, Rosalind, chose the academic route in pursuit of access to college. While he couldn't achieve the same success, Michael's fierce competitiveness to be the best at everything meant he still tried to beat his sister academically. It dragged Michael's grades up to beyond those of his peers also eyeing up college basketball scholarships.

It was another string to his bow that made Jordan attractive to colleges, but none had any interest in this boy from Laney. Wilmington in North Carolina was hardly a fertile scouting area for colleges, and few were looking in Jordan's direction while he was developing into an exceptional player.

The next season, Jordan made the Varsity team, but something even more important happened to him. It was what Michael, his coaches and his parents had literally been praying for; he shot up from 5 ft. 10 in. to 6 ft. 5 in. tall. He finally had the physical gifts that would allow him to play basketball at a college or professional level. Now it was time to see if he could develop the skills needed to make it in one of the most competitive sports on the planet.

Jordan's sophomore year was characterised by even more focus from Coach Herring. He worked on Jordan becoming more selfish and leading the team during games. Matches would be determined by whether Michael was having a good day or not – even when opposition coaches knew he was going to be the main point of attack, it was extremely difficult to stop him. He led the Laney High School Varsity team to one of its best seasons and was rewarded when the University of North Carolina called to ask him to join a trial training camp during the off season. It had become clear to their scouts that Jordan was a strong candidate for a scholarship to their college programme.

After Michael sufficiently impressed at the University of North Carolina training camp, he was invited to 'five-star' camp, which was held annually for the best high-school players in the nation. The ability he showed on this platform catapulted Michael from a small-town nobody to being widely recognised by college scouts and the media as one of the best prospects in the country. It took years of hard work for him to become an overnight sensation. Many colleges came calling, but it was North Carolina that Michael plumped for. His experience during their training camp before 'five-star' proved a crucial deciding factor.

Jordan still had his senior year of high school left, and desperately hoped to bring a state championship to his home town before he departed. The season started well, with six wins on the bounce. Having now shot to national fame, everyone seemed in awe of him, opponents and teammates alike. Michael was no longer a secret; every home game was packed to the rafters in the Laney School gym, with people 'queuing for hours' in the hope of being able to say they saw Michael Jordan in high school.

He would average 27.8 points per game that season, carrying Laney to a 19–4 record. The playoffs loomed large, and Michael's dream of bringing home a championship for his school seemed within his grasp. First up was New Hanover, a team who were great rivals of Laney but had already been defeated three times by Jordan and co.

Up six points with two minutes to go, it seemed Laney were in total control. But in a freak series of plays, the game turned on its head. The score became tied at 52–52. With seven seconds to go, the ball was in the hand of the man of the moment, Michael Jordan. He made a move, went for a jump shot to win the game – but was penalised by the referee for an offensive foul. To compound the issue, Jordan was fouled out of the game, and he watched from the bench as New Hanover made the subsequent free throws to advance to the next round. The dream for Jordan was over.

Gattison, one of the leading players for opponents New Hanover that day and someone who is a close friend of Jordan, has never mentioned this match to Michael ever again – despite the pair's tendency to trash talk. He knew how deeply the loss wounded him; it is something he has held on to ever since.

Michael would progress to North Carolina University, become a superstar in the college leagues and then light up the NBA in a way that arguably no one else ever has. He would finish his career with a staggering 6 NBA Champions rings, 6 NBA Finals MVP awards, 5 overall NBA MVP awards and 14 appearances in the NBA All-Star Team.[10] During his professional career, Michael's competitive edge would become legendary. While it was initially thought that trash-talking and facing off one-on-one against opponents was a tactic Jordan used to fire himself up, it quickly became obvious this was an integral part of him. His competitiveness and tenacity remained strong even after his career in sport had finished, not least in the establishment of the Jordan brand with Nike.

The origins of the Michael Jordan who would make opponents quiver in their boots in the NBA began at his childhood home in Wilmington and continued to develop at Laney High School. When he started playing basketball in the front yard of his house, it was the competition with Larry as much as the sport itself that absolutely captivated a young Michael Jordan. The long battles out on the court were driven by Michael's need to beat his brother Larry, and his inability to do so. He enjoyed basketball, but the real fire was in proving his worth against his brother. It was the inception of the attitude that shaped Michael's many equally personal individual battles in the NBA with the likes of Clyde Drexler and Kobe Bryant. Every player he met from then on was another Larry to be beaten.

But Michael's response to his crushing defeats at the hand of his older brother should not be overlooked. What set Michael apart from most competitive kids is that rather than taking the defeats from Larry and giving up, Michael internalised the feeling and strived even harder to beat him. It would have been easy to go and play baseball, which he was having some success with, and leave Larry to play basketball just as his father had wanted. But he could not let Larry continue to beat him. This holding on to failure and redoubling his efforts is something that we see throughout Jordan's childhood. It is best demonstrated by the fact he still holds onto the pain of losing a high-school state semi-final. You would expect he could brush off this disappointment given how long ago it was, and the successes that Jordan would gone on to achieve, but it remains so sore that no one will talk to him about it. Defeat played a more critical role than any success that Jordan had.

One of the biggest reasons that Michael wanted to win so badly was his need to prove himself to his father – 'Just go in the house with the women.' This single line that questioned who Jordan was as a man laid the foundation for the fearsome edge that he would bring to the game. The personal nature of it during his childhood created a need in the mind of Jordan to better himself so that, at some point, he could become a version of himself that would be accepted.

How deeply he felt his failures as a child, and how competitive that made him, was the fire that propelled a good athlete like Jordan into the stratosphere of becoming the greatest basketball player ever. This competitive edge in every game, the burning desire to win that could not be matched either by his opposition or teammates, was the most defining factor in Jordan's childhood. It transformed an ordinary child into the competitor who would destroy opponents in the NBA.

Although Michael Jordan is an exceptional case of this competitiveness, it is a mentality trait that develops in every single champion's childhood. Each champion was deeply competitive and would feel a genuine sense of pain and anguish when they lost. It is for this reason that they would train countless hours and focus their entire lives on winning an event, regardless of whether it was a world championship final or a local swimming gala. The need to win, and beat the rest, was all-consuming. Competitiveness is a unifying factor that linked all of the champions in this book, an absolute necessity to reach the top.

The internalising of failure that we see so prominently in Jordan is also reflected in many of the champions in this book. They hold on to their losses for years and are able to respond to defeat in a very special way. Rather than giving up, they double down in their attempts to win and overcome their adversaries. Whereas it may be that some competitive children hate losing so much that they give up when they do fail, these champions were able to keep going despite disappointments.

When we think of competitiveness and internalising failure, Cristiano Ronaldo is not the first name that springs to mind. From the outside, Ronaldo can seem like a bit of a prima donna; constantly frustrated, he is prone to petulant outbursts akin to a young kid who's not getting their own way. It is far from the image just described of the never-give-up attitude of a young Michael Jordan. But on the 10th July 2016, the world saw a different side to Cristiano Ronaldo. They saw the burning competitiveness to win, no matter what.

Portugal were far from glamorous in their route to the Euro 2016 final, with a string of narrow, often dull victories progressing them from the groups through the knockout stages. The team was built on a tough defence and Ronaldo as the main threat going forward, providing them with the X factor that always gave them a chance of victory.

Playing against hosts France in the final, who had been in scintillating form, few backed Portugal to win. For Ronaldo, this game could not have been more important. Despite winning everything in club football, as well as multiple Ballon d'Or trophies for best player in the world, success with his country had eluded him. It was the missing piece in his glittering football CV. He had suffered heartache before, most notably in 2004 when Portugal had been favourites in the European Championship final, only to lose to rank outsiders Greece. It was international success that was going to cement Ronaldo's legacy as not just one of the best players in the world, but one of the best of all time.

In just the eighth minute of the game, Ronaldo felt a sharp pain in his knee after a challenge with Dmitri Payet.

Tears welled up in his eyes as he feared the worst. He tried to continue, but it became increasingly obvious that he was in no fit state to play. He hobbled on, leaving the pitch twice and coming back on, but failing to move freely enough to offer anything in attack. Eventually, he slumped to the floor, and was substituted in the 25th minute in floods of tears. In one of the biggest games of his career, Ronaldo had fallen foul of bad luck.

He sat on the bench, and the whole Portuguese team seemed deflated and slightly bewildered without their leader. The game continued with France dominating possession, but Portugal's stalwart defence kept them at bay. The game moved at a dreary pace, with no one from the French team able to provide the spark to break through the resolute Portuguese defence. The game entered extra time.

As the minutes ticked on, and the intensity increased, Ronaldo increasingly couldn't sit down.[11] He prowled the technical area, standing just behind coach Fernando Santos. He tried to kick every ball and win every challenge from the touchline, such was his desperation to win.

In the 109th minute, Portuguese striker Éder scored with an out-of-the-blue 25-yard strike that sent their fans, players and coaches into delirium. Ronaldo jumped up, almost exploding with joy. Despite having very little of the ball and few attacks, Portugal were minutes away from the title. The excitement in Ronaldo's face was obvious.

Ronaldo's touchline antics entered overdrive. He began instructing the players like a coach. He urged them on for one final effort, co-ordinating and cajoling, working alongside coach Fernando Santos to eek every last effort from them. He issued tactical instructions, encouragement and decision-making to his comrades on the pitch. He was still hobbling from the injury, but his enthusiasm and intensity was infectious. As the minutes ticked on, the hand movements of Ronaldo and Santos became more frantic, turning from hope to excitement. When the final whistle blew, the smile on Ronaldo's face was as big as anyone's. Mission complete, his place in history was cemented.

This episode showed a different side to Ronaldo to what we usual perceive his personality to be: selfish, narcissistic and petulant. Instead, we saw a competitive leader who was invested in his team's success, even when he couldn't play himself and be in the limelight. Similar to Jordan, it is his total competitiveness that lies at the core of Ronaldo's success. He has always wanted to be the best, even amongst his teammates. The Euro 2016 final showed a developing maturity to understand how he could use his competitiveness as a leader within a team.

Like Jordan, Cristiano hardly grew up in the epicentre of his sport – born on the Portuguese island of Madeira, he didn't even have a full-sized football pitch in his neighbourhood[12] – but a young Cristiano was rarely without a ball. He would play at every opportunity he could, which usually took the form of impromptu games on the streets against all comers, young and old. From the streets of Liverpool to the favelas of Rio, street football has always produced highly skilled, technical players. His signature style was developed on the roads around his home, where he would use short and fast movements to dodge and weave past older and bigger players.

His first club was CF Andorinha, a small local club based in his hometown of Santo António, Funchal.

Playing at the weekends for the club quickly became the focus of little Cristiano's life. His first coach, Francisco Afonso, said that even when Ronaldo joined as a nine-year-old, 'Football was what Cristiano lived for ... and whenever he couldn't play or missed a game he was devastated'.

Ronaldo's competitiveness became clear extremely early in his footballing development. Andorinha Club President Rui Santos in particular recalls a game against Camacha, one of the strongest teams on the island, when Ronaldo was still very young. At halftime, Andorinha were losing 2–0, and:

> Ronaldo was so distraught that he was sobbing like a child who's had his favourite toy confiscated. In the second half he came onto the pitch and scored two goals, leading the team to a 3–2 victory. He definitely did not like to lose. He wanted to win every time and when they lost he cried.[13]

Even then, his competitive streak was an important driving force. Not only did he hate to lose, but he managed to affect the game enough to prevent it.

His antics led to his first nickname; albeit not a positive one. Former teammate Ricardo Santos describes how 'Cristiano really liked winning. When that didn't happen, Ronaldo cried. So much so that he had the nickname "crybaby"'.[14]

Against the bigger teams, who were considerably better than Andorinha, it was obvious that Ronaldo's team would lose. Cristiano simply didn't want to play, such was his hatred of defeat. Despite his son's wishes, Cristiano's father, Jose, still made him take part. He told him that 'giving up was for the weak'. It taught him to be able to deal with losses and, instead of giving up, improve to come out on top. It was the same formative moment of facing up to defeat and working harder that Michael Jordan developed during his one-on-ones against his brother Larry.

His success on the island of Madeira led Ronaldo to attract the attention of some of the scouts from the professional academies in Portugal. Cristiano was invited to a trial at Sporting Lisbon, one of the two biggest teams in the country. Cristiano had never been on a plane before, and the trip to the mainland was a brand new experience.

Despite his nervousness about travelling, he felt at home once he stepped on the pitch at the Sporting Lisbon academy. Within minutes in his first session, his dribbling, speed and agility stood out from the other academy youngsters, and the coaches clearly saw that he was a special talent.

After making this good initial impression, Academy Director Aurelio Pereria came to watch him. Ronaldo quickly impressed the top boss too: 'He was talented, he could play with both feet, he was incredibly fast and when he played it was as if the ball was an extension of his body', says Pereria. 'But what impressed me more was his determination. His strength of character shone through. He was courageous – mentally speaking he was indestructible.'

Despite all the technical skills developed on the streets of Madeira, it was his mental qualities that shone through the most.

His competitiveness and desperate desire to win was different from the others, even at the elite junior level. The director and coaches were so enamoured with him that the club decided to spend €22,500 to bring the 12-year-old Ronaldo to the academy. This was an unbelievable sum for someone so young, but the coaches were convinced by the huge potential they had seen.

It was time for Ronaldo to relocate to Lisbon. A completely new life for someone who was barely a teenager was tough to adjust to. It was a culture shock - he was moving to a city he didn't know and had to adapt to an entirely new way of living, with coaching at the academy being juggled alongside school lessons and leisure time.

One of the key figures in guiding him through this period was Leonel Pontes, who accompanied him to training and to school. "'Ronaldo was decisive in everything he did" he recalls, "He wanted to be the best at everything – table tennis, tennis, pool, table football, darts, athletics – he wanted to beat every opponent, be the fastest. He had to win no matter what sport he was playing. I think one of the reasons he got to where he is today is because he always wanted more.'" [15]

Biographer Luca Caioli recalls how Ronaldo separated himself from his teammates:

> They find him in the gym at 1am lifting weights without permission. He does press-ups and sit-ups in the dorm and trains with weights around his ankles to improve his dribbling. When his teammates head for the showers after training sessions, he stays on the pitch, practising free kicks against life-sized targets.[16]

Here was someone who wanted to be the best, suddenly in a supportive environment that gave him all the tools he needed. He flourished.

Ronaldo himself is fully aware of how important competition is to his character:

> I'm a competitive person and that's never going to change. Obviously, I'm growing up and becoming more mature. But the way I think doesn't change.
>
> I've already won everything there is to win, but I'll never stop trying to win until the day I retire. That's just who I am. My aim, my ambition, is to be the best. Ultimately, if I come within reach of being the best, then great – although what I'd really love is to go down as one of the best players in history.[17]

From his first coach at nine years old to the academy coaches at Sporting Lisbon, it was Ronaldo's competitiveness they noticed as his standout attribute. Time and again, they reference his incredible desire to win every game, shown perhaps most by his emotional outbursts when he lost. His need to be the best ran so deep that he was prepared to do what others would not. Ronaldo would go above and beyond to improve himself, because he was competitive not just from a team perspective, but also individually against his peers. He always had this slightly selfish attitude of wanting to personally be the best. It has made some fans dislike him, but as a child it was crucial to pushing his boundaries, both physically and mentally.

Undoubtedly, Ronaldo's childhood mentality was vital for developing into the player who would become a world superstar. Ronaldo and Jordan's stories show that coaches at the highest levels noticed their competitiveness, drive and determination more so than their obvious technical skills or physical attributes. Their mental attributes, the way they thought and, subsequently, competed with opponents, was unlike the other prodigies they were assessing at Sporting Lisbon's academy or the 'five-star' training camp for high-school basketball prospects.

They carried this throughout their lives. Both athletes' professional careers are crammed full of stories where they were still trying their heart out in the dying embers of matches. Matches where the Chicago Bulls are winning by 20 points but Jordan was still intent on racking up baskets, or Real Madrid leading 4–0 and still Ronaldo desperately trying to score. Often, fans can't understand this, but their competitiveness is not something that can be turned off. It is part of them.

Both Ronaldo and Jordan as children did not obviously stand out in terms of their physical attributes. Early coaches instead commented on their burning competitiveness as the key way that they were different from other children. Common to all the champions is that their childhood was shaped by a similar burning competitiveness. It is an absolute necessity for sporting success, and it is the first building block in helping us understand the Champion Mindset.

Although providing the cornerstone of the Champion Mindset, competitiveness is not enough motivation itself. How did our champions maintain motivation to engage in the practice and performances needed for success over the long term?

2

Motivation

To consider what else motivates our champions, we need to think back to their very first moment in the sport. Most are introduced by a friend or family who plays the sport themselves. But what makes them decide to play it again and eventually seek out some way of playing it regularly? That immediate, infectious desire to want to play the game more is due to interest in sport. After more exposure, this can develop into a passion for the sport; one of the core motivations for our champions during their childhood.

In her autobiography, *Paula*,[1] female marathon world record holder Paula Radcliffe writes:

> I don't remember a time in my life when I didn't run... Running down the lane behind our house to meet Dad as he returned from his training run... Aged 4, I would scamper off, not stopping or slowing until I reached him. Without drawing breath I would then turn and run alongside him all the way back to the house. Even then running was fun.[2]

Paula Radcliffe has loved to run for as long as she can remember. She would run whenever she could. She raced against her brother, two years her senior, along the beach during their summer holidays. At primary school, she would head off running together with a friend. However, it was her runs with her father that she treasured the most.

Paula's favourite moment of the week was when she accompanied her father running through the forest. Most weekends he would complete a long run there, the weekly ritual of nearly all club runners. Towards the end of the run, he would be joined by his young daughter, who would run with him for as long as she could. Paula would keep going at his pace till she hit utter exhaustion, seeing how long she could stay by his side.

Obviously, Paula's breathless running alongside her dad had developed her running ability from a young age. But more important for her future career than the training (of which plenty was going to come over the rest of her childhood years) was the sheer joy she felt when running.

> It isn't just the competition that appeals to me. Running is something I enjoy, full stop. Being out in a nice part of the countryside, running fast, the breeze in your face, feeling free and just seeing how long you can keep going. There is the sense of escape from the real world, the exhilaration that comes when you run hard, the search to see how far you can push yourself, just being at one with yourself: they are all part of why I love running.[3]

Her father also helped Paula when she began racing.

Paula finished second in her first cross-country race at school, and showed the competitiveness needed for success. 'I was really annoyed because this girl beat me – I was only about eight or nine – so my dad took me to a little circuit every Saturday for four weeks and taught me how to run downhill and just relax more and let my body go. On the next race I got away from her on the downhill.'[4]

Aged 11, Paula travelled from home in Bedford to watch her father run the London Marathon. As she waited for her dad to pass, someone else caught her attention: Norwegian runner Ingrid Kristiansen on her way to smashing the women's world marathon record in a time of 2:21:06. 'It broke down any barriers I had in my head', says Paula Radcliffe. 'I thought: why can't I be in there running and being competitive too?'[5] It cemented the competitive mindset that was required for her to be successful.

Although the competitiveness was clearly there, the heart of the motivation for Paula came from the very act of running. Her intrinsic love for her sport meant that it was never hard to find the desire to train as it was one of her favourite things to do. Paula would see going out for a run as a reward, not a chore. When her homework and house duties were dealt with, she would be allowed to go out and train. This 'reward system', with running as her treat, was something Paula continued right through her childhood and during her university days. In exchange for studying, she would get to run. It wasn't until she became a fully-fledged professional that running truly became the core activity of her day.

Paula rarely missed training because she didn't want to. It fitted in perfectly with her coach Alex Stanton's theory that he never forced anyone to train; you had to have the desire to want to do the work, otherwise there was no point. Her passion for running, combined with her competitiveness, helped her maintain this training throughout difficult periods during her childhood.

As you would expect, many of our sporting champions loved their sports greatly at the beginning of their childhood, just like Paula. But this was not entirely uniform. Michael Phelps hated getting into the water for the first time and would make up any excuse to get out of his swimming class.[6] Usain Bolt did not really enjoy sprinting in the same way that he loved cricket and football.[7] They loved winning but they did not draw their main motivation from the intrinsic nature of their sport.

We also see cases where, after the playful love of a sport motivated a child to play for hours in their youth, they grow to seriously dislike their sports as adults. A case that has caught the headlines is the wonderfully skilled Australian tennis player Nick Kyrgios.[8]

Once Kyrgios decided to focus solely on tennis aged 14, he flew through the junior ranks, including winning two junior major titles. He was a refreshing and exciting addition to the professional game, and in 2014 truly captured the imagination of the tennis public during Wimbledon. He defeated the likes of Rafael Nadal and Richard Gasquet with an audacious, aggressive playing style that took him to the quarter-finals. It was clear to all that this was someone who could be one of the best in the world.

But since then, his career has been characterised by a series of hopeful moments mixed with disappointment. This has been largely due to his inability to stay motivated. The toll of competing at the professional level is something Kyrgios has struggled with, even throwing away games mid-match. In 2016, he was fined $16,500 and banned for eight weeks after purposefully losing a match in the second round of the Shanghai Rolex Masters. He lost to Mischa Zverev 6–3 6–1, at one point asking the umpire: 'Can you call time so I can finish this match and go home?'[9]

On another occasion, he openly questioned his own dedication: 'There are players out there that are more dedicated, that want to get better, that strive to get better every day, the one-percenters. I'm not that guy.'[10]

This lack of motivation drives fans and coaches mad. He has been widely derided for it, but sadly the process of training, travel and a near continuous year-round pro tour circuit seems to have taken all joy out of tennis for him. As a result, the motivation to make it to the top is simply not there.

As we will look at in more detail later in this book, practice for the champions is very strenuous and, often, not much fun. It is repetitive, mentally straining, difficult work. This can often beat the life out of any love for the game, and only a few (such as Paula Radcliffe) truly love their sport throughout their entire career. Many rekindle that love in later life when the spotlight is turned away and the practice hours are not necessary.

But if a childhood spent practising a sport tends to diminish the love for it, something must replace that love in order to keep the athlete going. What fills the gap as the amount of play reduces and serious work increases? Fortunately, another form of motivation is at hand. Many athletes describe becoming aware of it in a 'penny drop' moment, often occurring in their mid-teens: early successes lead to a desire to be great, and to have the fame and glory associated with being a champion.

Children begin to realise what being a champion could

mean for their lives, namely status within society, huge amounts of money and sponsorship, and an opportunity to make history. A certain event often triggers this thought process; and once it has stuck, it is something that can motivate them throughout their youth. It can make the difference between staying with the sport or quitting.

As well as this realisation of what can be achieved in sport, equally powerful is the belief from the child that they can get there. It requires self-confidence to be able to look at a difficult challenge like being the best in the world at anything and think that you can go out and achieve it. Armed with the self-confidence developed by those around them, the dream often leads them to focus everything in their young lives towards being the best; an all-consuming motivator that drives them for years on end. There are very few other occupations in society where a person's entire life points towards a single goal that is extremely difficult to attain. It is this desire to do something great that often provides significant motivation.

Desire for fame and glory is perhaps best demonstrated in Muhammad Ali. He was born on 17th January 1942 in Louisville.[11] According to his parents, both Ali and his younger brother were polite and well behaved and never gave them too much trouble. He wasn't one of the best at school and seemed a fairly ordinary child by all accounts. But in October 1954, the fighter awoke inside him.

Ali and a friend rode their bicycles to the Columbia Auditorium, which was hosting an annual black bazaar called 'The Louisville'. After attending the event, he stepped outside to head home only to find that his red-and-white Schwinn bike had been taken. Ali got into a rage. He announced to everyone that he was going to find the bike thief and 'whup his ass'.

After being told by a passer-by of the whereabouts of a policeman, Ali headed over to report the incident. The policeman in question was Joe Martin, who was at the time coaching at his boxing gym. He quipped to Ali that 'If you are going to whup his ass, you are first going to have to learn how to fight'.

You have to wonder whether the thief of a young boy's bike knows the profound impact he had on the history of sport by introducing Muhammad Ali to boxing. Ali began training in the ring, and quickly took to the sport. He worked hard under the tutelage of Martin and began competing on the vibrant Kentucky junior boxing scene. Despite being knocked down and taking a few losses in his early days, a young Ali kept coming back for more. His focus on improvement was laser-like. He trained six days a week in the gym, and never drank or smoked a cigarette.

Joe Martin says Ali was unlike any other kid he had trained:

> He stood out because, I guess, he had more determination than most boys, and he had the speed to get him someplace. He was a kid willing to make the sacrifices to achieve something worthwhile in sports. I realized it was almost impossible to discourage him. He was easily the hardest worker of any kid I ever taught.[12]

Another upcoming Louisville boxer Jimmy Ellis remembers his attitude:

> He wanted to box and he wanted to be great, and that's what his life was all about. I

> never saw him fight in the streets. I never saw him pushing or shoving outside the ring. But in the gym, he took his boxing very seriously.[13]

It wasn't long before Ali was dreaming of bigger and better things for himself and his family. Often, mothers are worried about their kids getting involved in boxing, but Muhammad's felt he could handle himself: 'He had confidence in himself, and that gave me confidence in him. He started boxing when he was twelve, and he'd tell me how someday he'd be champion of the world.'[14]

Throughout his career, Ali would tell anyone and everyone about how great he would become. Even in those early days, the fame, the glamour and the money were major motivators for the young boy from Louisville putting in the hours in the gym.

> When I started boxing, all I really wanted was someday to buy my mother and father a house and own a nice big car for myself. I figured if I could turn pro and get on Saturday night fights, I could make four thousand dollars just for one night.
>
> Then my dreams started to grow.
>
> In school, sometimes I'd pretend they were announcing my name over the loudspeaker system, saying 'Cassius Clay, Heavyweight Champion of the World'. Other times, I'd draw a picture of a jacket on a piece of paper, like a high-school football jacket; only on the back of the jacket I'd write 'National Golden Gloves Champion' or 'Cassius Clay, World Heavyweight Champ'.[15]

Of course, what made Muhammad Ali special was his

ability to walk the walk as well as talk the talk. Ali's amateur career would see him go on to win eight Kentucky Golden Gloves and two national championships. One of the national championship wins gave him the chance to go to the 1960 Rome Olympics in the Light-Heavyweight division. He would dominate the field and dazzle the crowd on his way to gold, capturing the attention of the mainstream US media. It was the inception of a star who would grace boxing on the professional scene for the next two decades.

Ali didn't choose to reject the usual path of childhood and instead spend his life in the gym because of an all-consuming love of boxing, in the same way that Paula Radcliffe couldn't get enough of running. He wasn't a thug who just loved beating people up; as coach Joe Martin recalls, Ali never had any interest in fighting outside the ring. Instead, it was deeply related to his desire to be 'great'. He wanted to be a champion, he wanted to win titles and he wanted to make enough money to be able to make him and his family comfortable. A popular quote Ali made later in life was: 'I hated every minute of training, but I said "Don't quit. Suffer now and live the rest of your life as a champion".'[16] The training and the boxing didn't hold a great deal of allure to Ali – the opportunities associated with being a sports star did.

No account better illustrates how important greatness was to a teenage Ali than a story told by Bob Surkein, a referee who officiated a bout Ali won early in his amateur boxing career when he was still a kid:

> I remember, one time we were staying at a hotel for a tournament out-of-town. Cassius had won his first bout on a knockout. The next morning, I went down to the hotel coffee shop for a newspaper. I bought one, took it up

> to my room, and couldn't find the sports section. So I went back downstairs and there were ten or fifteen papers there; no sports sections. And I got to thinking. I said, 'I know where the damn sports sections are'. So I went up to Cassius's room, and he was sitting on the floor with a pair of scissors, cutting his picture out of all the sports sections where it had been that day.[17]

Seeing his picture in the paper was a real thrill for the young Muhammad Ali.

As in many aspects of his life, Ali was fairly unique in the extent to which glory motivated his introduction to the sport of boxing. The desire to be 'great', in terms of external validation such as titles or finances, tends to develop later in an athlete's childhood when they understand the potential and the enormity of what they can achieve in the sport.

This 'penny drop' moment comes in one of two main ways: when the youngster themselves get their first taste of success, or they are inspired by others achieving something phenomenal. For triathlete Jonny Brownlee, it was when his brother received his Great Britain team kit before representing his country at triathlon aged just 12.[18] He returned home, excited by the kit and representing his country, and realised his future could potentially be a career in triathlon. It also ignited the desire of his brother, Jonathan, which jealousy kicked in. Similarly, Phelps remembers the moment his coach sat him down and said he could reach the Olympics if he continued to work hard.[19] For others, it was seeing the Olympics for the first time, watching a world title bout or a World Cup final. All can have a transformative impact in offering a new way of motivating.

To the majority of us, this kind of 'fame and glory' motivation does not come naturally. To think you could one day be good enough to represent your country and to seriously spend your entire life pursuing it requires an audacity that most of us do not possess. But to actually execute it requires a maturity to be able to recognise the magnitude of what you are trying to achieve, and religiously work towards it as a goal – even if you are just a teenager. Putting in the short-term work to meet this long-term goal is crucial.

This is where the competitive edge as a motivator re-enters the story. Often it is this drive to beat your fellow competitors in every training session, in every race, that bridges the gap between pushing yourself in the short term while reaching for these long-term goals. Towards the end of a child's teenage years, with the thought of professional sport and world competitions firmly on their mind, it is this blend that drives them forward to commit practically all their time to their sport.

Alongside a competitive attitude, a complex blend of passion for the sport and desire for fame combine to complete the motivation puzzle. Usually, passion for the sport is crucial at the beginning of the journey for a child picking up the sport and can be a factor throughout a career. More often than not, the repetitiveness of training means passion is replaced with a desire for success and glory that fuels the drive to reach the top during the teenage years.

These three factors are what drive our champions during their childhood, and form the Champion Mindset. It is this mentality that distinguishes them from their peers and leads to separation from the pack, even at an elite level. When a child is also given the right prerequisites to thrive, they can be propelled towards sporting stardom. It is the shaping of this mindset that we will now look at in more detail.

We've established that, as children, future champions develop a distinctive Champion Mindset that differentiates them from other young athletes. This requires a high level of competitiveness, an ability to accept failure and utilise it to improve, and a motivation driven by a fluid mix of passion for the sport and a desire for fame and glory.

Having now looked at this mindset and how it exhibited itself in the actions of Michael Jordan, Cristiano Ronaldo, Paula Radcliffe and Muhammad Ali, we have a better understanding of *why* these champions succeeded through their childhood experiences. But *how* did they develop this mentality? What were the factors that allowed them to develop these mental attributes so far removed from ourselves?

The main contributors to developing this mindset are different for each champion. In general, the same figures are involved – coaches, parents, siblings, school, sporting institutions and networks. But, usually, it was one or two key individuals within these groups who primarily shaped their Champion Mindset. In the next chapters, we will look at for each of our champions, from Muhammad Ali to Lewis Hamilton, which figures featured most prominently in their lives to take them from ordinary backgrounds to extraordinary competition and look at what they did to develop the Champion Mindset.

3

Coaches

Typically at major championships, following the race the athletes are ushered to the media pen for immediate reaction. This being one of the biggest moments of their careers, where dreams have either been made or shattered, it is understandable that few can speak coherently and with clarity about what just happened to them. But, often, the first name to be thanked in the breathless words of the athlete is their coach. Arguably, by the time they are professional athletes, coaches have become as important as family to them. They spend a large amount of their time with their coaches and share hardships together in their attempts to reach the pinnacle of their sport. The bond can be one that lasts a lifetime, despite the inevitable tantrums and the arguments that are likely when you put two people together striving for a difficult goal.

Coaches always have been, and always will be, the bedrock in a child's sporting development; nothing is more critical to their progression; they provide the guidance, training and expertise required to help them progress. Undoubtedly, coaches are important actors in all our champions' childhood experiences, whether they were professionals, amateurs or parents. Defining what made a good coach for these athletes is what we will seek to understand better in this chapter.

Let's return to the childhood of the best female distance runner in history. After a young Paula Radcliffe was thrilled by breathlessly running after her dad through the forest, she wanted to follow her running passion and join an organised club.[1] Frodsham Harriers, a small rural athletics club close to the Radcliffe family home, provided her first experience of club running. Paula loved the camaraderie of it, and the fun they would have in their competitions during training sessions: 'It was at Frodsham Harriers that the running bug hit me, and though I would spend just two years with the club before moving with my family to Bedford, the connection with the people and the area has remained.'[2]

When the family moved to Bedford, a first priority for Paula was finding her another club. Paula's parents took her to Bedford & County Athletics Club, a well-respected local club with a large number of runners across all age brackets. On the first night that her father took her to the club, Paula was put into the group looked after by coaches Alex and Rosemary Stanton. Alex took responsibility for most of the formal coaching, while Rosemary took more of a supportive role and kept a beady eye out to ensure that discipline was maintained. To Paula on that first trip, Alex seemed nicer, whereas 'around Rosemary you were on your best behaviour'. The girls who were in the club were a tight group and Paula was welcomed in. She felt at home there.

Five months later, and after only a light training regime with the club, Paula made her first appearance in

The National Cross Country Championships. She was aged 11. Out of 606 competitors, she finished 299th, and took great pride in the result. Despite the team having mixed results, coach Alex came away with the belief that he could build a team to win the national championships. He saw potential in his girls, and felt he now just had to develop it. Alex subsequently ramped up the training in pursuit of this goal – with Paula moving from one to two training sessions a week.

He instilled a belief in his team of girls; a quiet, unshakeable confidence that they could reach this considerable goal. Yet Alex didn't pile the pressure on; he always focused on each and every one of them doing their best, regardless of whether that was a personal best in a lowly race or a national championship.

Alex simply loved the sport of running and, together with Rosemary, they were willing to make great sacrifices (both in terms of finances and time) to see their girls running well. Countless times, Paula's mum would drive her to Bedford Park early in the morning to train. She would always be greeted by Alex, on the bike and ready to follow her on her training run, regardless of weather conditions.

Despite this love for the sport, he maintained a healthy perspective on life balance. Alex would ask Paula about how her studies were developing, and whether there was anything that was bothering her. He provided a sounding board for any concerns that Paula had in her life. He was part of all the girls' lives. His view was a balanced one. 'When it came to a choice between homework and athletics, he would say homework had to come first,'[3] Paula recalls.

As the team completed their training and witnessed

the fruits of their labour, belief grew that they could pull off the impossible and become national champions. Sure enough, 12 months on, the efforts of Rosemary and Alex paid off. Bedford & County Athletics Club took The National Cross Country Championships title. Paula finished 4th and the second-best scorer in the team, showing a phenomenal improvement from the previous year's 299th. It was a huge example for the girls of where hard work and dedication could take you.

Following this success, Alex continued to help develop the team and the other athletes in the club. But Paula's improvement had caught his eye, and Alex's commitment to her personal development was particularly strong. Even when, in 1994, she suffered a stress fracture and could only do sessions in the pool, Alex was always there for encouragement, despite not being able to offer any coaching. This commitment helped to foster a relationship between Paula and the Stantons where she viewed them 'more like second parents' than coaches.

The belief from her second parents in how far she could go knew no boundaries. Early on in Paula's career as one of the girls at Bedford & County, Alex told her to 'Aim for the moon; even if you miss, you'll land among the stars'[4]. Alex and Paula have always aimed for the top, and after her National Cross Country Championships performance, they now were looking at a new goal competing internationally.

Paula continued to develop at a rapid rate and began competing on a stage that her coaching duo was also unaccustomed to. In 1991, as second finisher at the national championships, she qualified for the World Junior Cross Country Championships in Antwerp. At her first international race, she finished a very respectable 15th, and left delighted with her performance. But the gap from 15th to 1st seemed insurmountable. Paula felt that the winner, Kenyan Lydia Cheromei, seemed in a completely different race to her, such was the gulf between them in terms of speed and endurance.

Reminiscent of his year-long plan to help Bedford & County win The National Cross Country Championships just a few years before, Alex began to develop a plan to help Paula top the world in junior cross-country running. He took a methodical approach to the challenge: he took Cheromei's time and figured she had run between 3:05 and 3:10 minutes per kilometre. His single aim for the next year was to train Paula for the next World Junior Championships to be able to run at that pace. Paula remembers how the focus shifted to the biggest junior title of all. 'The 1992 World Junior Cross-Country Championships in Boston, Massachusetts, were the target and we were determined to get there fitter and better prepared than I had ever been in my life.'[5]

To get Paula to run at this speed was going to require both of them to stretch their abilities. Alex was open and willing to listen to both Paula and those outside his circle to understand different viewpoints and ideas on how to improve the training to reach that elite performance. His 'willingness to learn new things and embrace new ideas' was crucial to helping him develop as a coach as he began training an athlete at the elite level for the first time. Of course, Paula had always been talented, but to compete with the best in the world she was going to have to push herself like never before.

After a year of great training and racing, Paula and her team arrived in Boston cautiously excited at her potential for success. The conditions were hardly idyllic; there was a harsh winter wind and it was -10C. It had snowed earlier in the week and now hard, packed snow lay on the ground. Paula was focused only on the race, helped by Alex's almost surreal calmness and confidence. His gut instinct was good, and he simply told Paula to go out and run a great race. He felt she was good enough to win it.

The race began in a flurry of national kits, hats and gloves, all athletes trying to position themselves and adjust to the conditions. Eventually, four broke away in the second half of the race; Paula, her teammate Jenny Clague, reigning champion Lydia Cheromei and Chinese athlete Wang Junxia. With 400 metres to go and Paula holding a slender lead, she knew she would lose out in a final sprint. Instead, she gave everything in a final long push to try and clinch the title. Metre by metre her lead extended, and she began running away from the field. She crossed the line in first, the best female junior cross-county athlete in the world, an incredible achievement for a girl from Bedford.

She captured the British media's attention in that moment and would be a focus within British sport for years to come with her dominance in female distance running. Paula was unlike any distance runner anyone had ever seen.

Paula would finish her running career with three London Marathon wins, three New York Marathon wins, as a former World Marathon, Half Marathon and Cross Country Champion and as a European Champion at 10,000 metres and Cross Country. No British distance runner has matched these achievements.

But her crowning glory was her world record in the marathon, which is still held in 2018 some 16 years after it was set. When she began running in marathons in 2002, the world record was set at 2:18:47 by Catherine Ndereba of Kenya. In the Chicago marathon, she wiped a minute and a half off this time, before reaching the current mark at the 2003 London Marathon by posting an earth-shattering time of 2:15:25, a full two minutes quicker than the nearest competitor at the time.[6] No one has yet been able to surpass this.

Along every step of the way through Paula's incredible journey, her coach Alex Stanton was with her. He would remain Paula's 'first coach and my only coach' for her entire running career. She never wavered from him, and never decide to move on to another, despite plenty of higher-calibre candidates wanting to work with someone of her ability. Instead, she stayed with Alex, the coach of Bedford & County Athletics Club, through good times and bad. His quiet, calm and confident demeanour was a great fit for Paula throughout her junior career, from her first session at Bedford & County through to the incredible World Junior Cross Country Championship victory. This attitude was the perfect foil for one of the major factors that seemed to count against Paula; her pre-race nerves. Always a calm voice, Alex would ground her and help unlock her potential in the race.

Beyond that, Alex's ambition for Paula from early on in her career helped to ensure that she aimed for the top of junior running. He truly wanted all his athletes to be the best that they could be – and rather than just thinking this, he took very specific plans and actions to make this happen. When targeting the national championships, Alex asked Paula to move up to two training sessions a week. For the worlds, a structured plan to get the required training in around school commitments was put in place. Translating aspirations into firm actions was a classic example of the role that a skilled coach can have.

The journey they shared from club running to international success during Paula's teenage years meant that the trust between them ran deep. The relationship was so strong that Paula always followed what Alex told her to do; even if she disagreed. They would debate her schedule, with Paula usually wanting to do more training, but whatever was agreed, Paula would never train behind Alex's back.

Paula's relationship with Alex, and the way they worked together, was as important as his technical skills as a coach. Alex could improve his technical skills through understanding different viewpoints on how to train at an elite level, something which he had not done before. What was much more difficult to replicate was the deep trust and synchronicity with which they worked together. Ultimately, Alex's relationship with Paula from childhood proved the crucial factor in maintaining their partnership throughout her career.

This trusting and understanding relationship allowed her to compete to the best of her ability with the knowledge of the safety net from her 'second parents'. This supporting environment allowed her to flourish and explore her love for running and competition. In other words, it enabled her to be competitive, motivated and learn from her failures – and ultimately to develop the Champion Mindset.

Despite also training another of the greatest athletes of all time who redefined their sport, Bob Bowman could not have been more different from Alex Stanton in his style and approach to coaching. As much as Alex was calm and considerate, Bob was demanding and energising. His influence on turning a physically gifted Michael Phelps into the best junior swimmer of all time was just as impressive as Alex's work with Paula.

Even as a toddler, Michael Phelps had always been

around swimming pools. His sister was a keen swimmer who was progressing well competitively. When he was seven years old, it was time for Michael to learn to swim, a requirement stipulated by his mother. Phelps hated the idea of swimming and did not want to learn, but his mum made him go to a stroke clinic class taught by a friend of hers.[7]

At the first session, Phelps tried every excuse to get out of the swimming lesson. He wanted nothing less than to get in that pool. But against the stubbornness of his mum, nothing would work. When he got in, it wasn't much better; he simply didn't like putting his face under the water. Unfortunately for Michael, quitting was not an option when under the tutelage of coach Cathy. She had a checklist, and Phelps had to learn all of it, one way or another. Eventually, he completed the list.

After a few more sessions in the pool, Phelps began to enjoy swimming. It began to feel like somewhere in Phelps' difficult childhood where he was in control and could be successful. He quickly progressed and started putting in more practice to try and improve. Then, just as his practice was beginning to show in his performances, Bob Bowman came along and altered the trajectory of his improvement to stratospheric.

Bob had a specific way of coaching, a well-defined list of rules and principles, and he wasn't about to change it for anyone. He was a coach who would demand 'sportsmanship, accountability and responsibility'. In his coaching philosophy, attitude was central to success, and was seen as the underpinning sporting development. North Baltimore Aquatics Club (NBAC), the club he coached for, would reward perfect attendance with a yellow cap that said in blue letters '100 per cent. Never Settle for Less'. Phelps was unsurprisingly always wearing that cap.

Phelps has always been intensely competitive about everything. He always wanted to win, but he absolutely hated to lose, whether it was who was first at the dinner table or a race at the end of a training session in the pool. Bob immediately saw that Phelps had the physical gifts to be a great swimmer; his height, the shape of his body, and the fact he was double-jointed in many limbs meant he had the raw potential to be a national or even international swimmer. Combined with this intensive competitive drive and work ethic, he was the prospect Bob had been waiting for.

Bowman pushed Phelps hard. He quickly understood that Phelps responded well to this kind of coaching. Bob took advantage of the drive that burned inside Michael by setting increasingly difficult expectations. Phelps remembers that 'Bob used to say to me: Let's see what you've got in you; use all the gas in the tank'.

Bob had to be creative just to produce sessions hard enough to challenge Michael who, entering his teenage years, was becoming the most remarkable swimming talent he had ever seen. "'I've always tried to find ways to give him adversity in either meets or practice and have him overcome it." Bowman has said. "The higher the level of pressure, the better Michael performs. As expectations rise, he becomes more relaxed... That's what makes him the greatest."'[8]

However, it was far from an easy relationship. Stories of the fights between the two are legendary – Bob kicking in the doorframe at NBAC and having full-blown screaming matches in the middle of practices.[9] Back in the early days, the biggest punishment Bob handed out to Phelps for not adhering to what he wanted was to simply end his training session and stop him swimming. He would have to sit at the side of the pool, waiting for his mum to finish work and pick him up.

Remaking Phelps' strokes at the age of 12 was a particularly notable battle between athlete and coach. Phelps had developed some niggling bad habits in his stroke that needed to be rectified before they became even more ingrained. Bob devised many drills to fix this, but Michael would push back from Bob's teaching and would sometimes lapse into bad technique. Always believing it was Phelps purposefully doing this, he would be thrown out of the practice. The moment that changed Phelps' swimming technique was when Bowman told him that he wasn't old enough or mature enough to accept criticism and change. In response to this, Phelps strove to prove him wrong.

That the process of improvement was hard and difficult was built into Bob's mantras. His philosophy was to set high goals and to 'work conscientiously, every day, to achieve them'. He was a full believer that you had to do what others were not prepared to do to be the best, particularly in a field such as swimming that was intensively competitive. The focus with which teenage Michael Phelps pursued goals under the coaching of Bowman was incredible; he would complete the intensive regime set by Bob and literally practise every day to do so.

Bob was so ambitious with Phelps that he sought to influence other areas of his young life to focus them towards swimming. In August 1997, with Phelps aged 12, Bowman sat down with him and his mum. He told them that Phelps could make the Olympics, possibly in three years (but definitely in seven), if he implemented a specific plan to do this. He had to drop other sports he was playing, like baseball and lacrosse, and move to a school that was prepared to accommodate his schedule. Michael's mum thought he was crazy.

What no one knew was that Bowman was actually underestimating Phelps' phenomenal potential. Phelps would not only make his Olympics debut aged 15 at Sydney 2000, but finish 5th in the 200-metre Butterfly. Four years later, he would compete in Beijing and take six golds and two bronze medals, beginning a haul that would finish in 2016 with a staggering 28 Olympics medals (23 golds) and has set 39 world records.[10]

Throughout his career, the tumultuous relationship between Bob and Michael has led to Phelps trying to sever the relationship multiple times.[11] But, it seems they simply cannot; in some way, they are both dependent on each other. After Athens, Phelps knew he had to leave Baltimore for his development. But leaving Bob, at the age of 18, was not an option. His childhood ties to his coach, the main male role model in his life, was not an option. Phelps was acutely aware of this:

There was no way I was leaving Bob. He was my coach, yes. But he was also much, much more. A friend, yes, but still more than that. Bob had changed not only how I swam but who I was as a person, reminding me constantly how much love and dedication he has for the sport and everyone in it. I don't think either one of us, to be honest, could do without the other for any length of time. I certainly wasn't about to try.[12]

Phelps did not have a father who was around a great deal to help bring him up. Bob, as coach and a strong male figure in his life, helped to fill that gap in his life. 'Bowman taught him not only discipline but also how to do up his tie before his first school dance, and how to drive.'[13] They argued and they fought but, ultimately, their two mentalities were very compatible. That's why Phelps has never been able to work with anyone else.

Bowman was undoubtedly one of swimming's greatest coaches and would go on in 2016 to become the US Olympic Swimming Team's head coach. In his book *The Golden Rules*,[14] he distils down his philosophy to *The Method*, '10 steps to world-class excellence in your life and work'. Bowman sees spreading the word of how to be successful as 'part of my personal mission: to help people realize that the best moments in our lives are built around achieving every day, and long-lasting, excellence'.[15]

We've looked at the stories of two of the great sporting athletes of all time and their polar-opposite coaches. Whereas Alex Stanton struck a reconciliatory tone in his coaching that would heavily involve Paula Radcliffe in the decision-making from a young age, Bob Bowman's role was to push Michael Phelps to his considerable limits. However, both helped to develop athletes that were true trailblazers in their sports.

Crucially, it was the personality match between the child and coach that was vital to both partnerships' success. Paula Radcliffe admitted that, alongside the stubbornness and competitiveness that would come to define her career in the marathon, she is also 'sensitive, self-conscious; a little vulnerable. Part of that is a yearning to be liked and to be accepted, and that has always been there'. Alex's support and encouragement during her teenage years when difficulties with friends loomed large was as important as the training. Alex became a rock to Paula throughout her career and gave her the confidence to go out and train to the best of her ability.

In comparison, Phelps talks about his hyper-competitive attitude as a kid. His mother ensured that all of her kids had 'goals, drive and determination. We were going to strive for excellence, and to reach excellence you have to strive at it and work for it'. He also believes his intensely competitive attitude is partially inherited from his father. Bowman saw both of these qualities in Michael and pushed him to his limits in these facets. He would constantly challenge Phelps with practically impossible goals, always pushing the boundary of what Phelps believed himself he could achieve. This was the best way to get the most out of him. It meant that sometimes they clashed but, ultimately, led to a productive partnership that produced the world's greatest ever swimmer.

It is unlikely that if both these coaches had swapped athletes, the same attitudes would have worked. The importance was that each coach's attitude suited the athlete, and the approach to training was specific to each individual. The outcome? A trusting relationship that ran so deep between coach and athlete that the athlete's childhood coach continued throughout their career.

This is a clear trend amongst our champions. Nearly all have only one or, at most, a few coaches that they work with throughout their careers. This is because the relationship is so important to the quality of training. Understanding the athlete's needs, attitude and behaviours is an important part of the coach's role in delivering top-quality training. Instead of leaving for a coach with better skills, often the coach grows with the child to learn new ways of working at the elite level. Building a relationship is as important as the development of technical skills, if not more so.

Academic studies have also helped to show this trend. The University of Washington ran an experiment training

Little League Baseball coaches to enhance their relationship skills with children. It found that the coaches were evaluated more positively by the players, particularly those with low self-esteem. All players had higher self-esteem compared to the control group.[16] A similar study later found that attrition was also significantly less – only 5 per cent of players left the next year compared to 26 per cent in the control group.[17]

Sophia Jowett from the School of Sport and Exercise at Loughborough University highlights that the research leans towards communication as the vital factor in building effective trusting relationships:

> A series of qualitative case studies that we have conducted over the last five years (e.g. Jowett & Cockerill, 2003) shows that communication is an important unifying relational component... Particularly in youth sport, communication that evolves around spontaneous dialogues of daily activities related to school and training has been shown to form the basis for developing trust in the coach (Timson, Katchis & Jowett, 2004). Thus, coaches that create opportunities for talk and disclosure related to the athletes' daily activities are more likely to develop trustworthy coach–athlete relationships.[18]

This viewpoint on coaching also helps to explain why so many of the parents in this book were also effective coaches of their children. Having been there since Day 1, the parents of course have a great insight into the behaviour of the child and understand how to get the best out of them. Given this, they are then able to fill in the technical skills they are missing.

Richard Williams, Serena and Venus Williams' father, is a perfect case in point. Despite having no prior knowledge of tennis, having never played in his life, he set to work learning the game. Following this, he looked into multiple coaching methodologies, and talked to local professionals.[19] After digesting all the material he could, he began to train his daughters, with the relationship already there. They developed an even closer and loving relationship, that helped Richard get the best quality training out of his daughters. Of course, both developed incredibly fast. Even in later times when professional coaches were brought in following their move to Florida, Richard remained the primary coach who would have the final say on any decisions.

Which brings us to another key attribute: all the champions commented their coaches were great learners. All read widely, considered many different methodologies and were willing to change their plans if other viewpoints proved to offer better results. This provides further support that these coaches were giving high-quality training sessions, as their basis for techniques were from the very frontier of current understanding of coaching. It is no coincidence that it was passionate, driven coaches who were great learners – a study in Australian elite sport coaches found that these personal factors in coaches (passion for the sport, drive to be the best) were vital to determining the extent to which coaches were willing to learn.

There is one major conflict that we must address when considering coaching. We have talked earlier about the need for constant coaching during practice, and also that the coaching must be of a high quality. This naturally brings about a financial implication. Given the huge number of hours needed to be dedicated, it seems incredible that anyone can afford the investment of money required for their child's development.

In truth, it is the kindness of coaches and perhaps their own aspirations to be successful that mean that coaches are practically never paid for their time coaching. In particular for children, sports coaches are often willing to go above and beyond their stipulated training hours. Their love for the sport runs so deep that it seems entirely natural for them to dedicate so much time, effort and even finances to help children develop their potential in the sport, and this is frequently done for little or no gain; it is only in the extreme cases of champions that widespread recognition and congratulations are given to the coaches.

Volunteering is one of the more curious aspects of sport, but it is one that continues to make it a special aspect of our lives. In few other fields are so many unpaid hours donated by selfless individuals who do so for the enjoyment and aspirations of children. It remains at the very heart of why so many people engage with and love sport from a young age.

Coaching is therefore about understanding the child and their attitudes, as much as having the technical skills to teach sport. This enabled coaches to know how best to push talented athletes like Paula Radcliffe and Michael Phelps, helping them progress quickly through junior ranks. However, it is also vital that coaches are avid learners themselves, spending time reading and talking to other coaches to learn and be at the frontier of knowledge to ensure the best quality training is given. This rare blend can lead to a lifelong relationship, the benefits of which extend well beyond the boundaries of the sport itself.

4

Parents

'We need to make two more kids and make them into tennis superstars.'[1]

For many, purposefully having children in order to raise them into tennis superstars is borderline insane. But perhaps even more shocking is that these two children became Serena and Venus Williams, two of the greatest female tennis players ever to grace the game, winning 33 majors between them (and counting). Richard Williams expertly executed his plan to raise them as tennis players from birth and managed to help his girls reach the pinnacle of one of the most competitive sports while they were still teenagers.

The quest to become international tennis superstars took over the Williams family's life to a greater extent than any other athlete studied in this book. The story of their success can be traced back to the childhood of not Serena and Venus Williams, but their father.

Richard Williams was born in Shreveport, a small

town in Louisiana. His childhood could hardly have been more difficult. In his autobiography *Black and White*,[2] Richard recounts how he was supported by his single mum, and how the family barely had enough money to survive – with Richard having to go to school without shoes and often with an empty belly. In the midst of this extreme poverty, Richard was deeply affected by the race divisions that defined life in Louisiana, getting involved in numerous clashes with the Ku Klux Klan at a young age.

His uncle, Roman Metcalf, worked in Chicago and always returned to Shreveport in a big car like a real hotshot. Richard wanted a piece of that. So, in December 1960, in a bid to get there, he jumped illegally into a boxcar on a freight train as it passed Shreveport. He curled up into the corner with just the clothes on his back and hoped no one would see him. Incredibly, on arrival in Chicago, he managed to find his uncle despite not having an address. He began living and working in the city alongside him as a construction worker. In his spare time, for the first time in his life, he had access to a library and developed a voracious appetite for reading, learning about business and finance. Due to a lack of career progression, terrible accommodation and being subject to the same segregation and suppression of race he had experienced in Louisiana, Richard became disillusioned with Chicago and the city quickly turned into a hell for him.

It was time for a change of direction, and to begin anew somewhere else. Now, with a little more money in his pocket, he headed west. Richard Williams again got on a freight train and hopped off on the outskirts of Los Angeles. This time, he had a clear vision of what he wanted to do. 'I had a plan. First, I would raise my level of education. Second, I would start my own business. My value would be what I created. I would live by my own judgment. I would accept no limits.'[3]

The fire of ambition burned strongly in Richard Williams. He moved into Compton with distant family and began looking for a job. But temptation was rife. Richard remembers 'it would have been easy to rob, steal, and cheat, or to use racism as an excuse for violence. It would have been equally easy to become a slave to drugs or alcohol and slowly turn into a zombie like so many other black men. I refused.'[4]

He maintained his self-discipline, and got a job working in a car wash. He moved on to a job working for IBM in a data-processing centre, before working for a bank.

It was here that he saw the opportunity to set up his own business. When he saw the maintenance team coming in at night to clean the bank at the end of his shift, he saw the quality of work they were doing. Richard believed he could do better. He duly opened the 'White Glove Maintenance Company', licensed in Sacramento, California. Soon he had contracts cleaning premises for three businesses and began hiring a number of employees: 'But I wasn't content with just making a living. I wanted more. I had ambition.'[5]

In the mid-1970s, Richard sold his maintenance company and moved on. He continued to play around with ideas for new businesses before eventually setting up a security company. In the downtrodden neighbourhood of Compton where he lived, there was a desperate need for security of anything valuable. But the current service offerings were poor, often scared away immediately by the presence of gangs. Richard set out to build a proper security business. They earned significant money, and moved to a house in Long Beach, very close to the beach itself. It was a large home, with enough space for his new family that he had married into by marrying Oracene, who had three daughters.

But despite his success in this business, Richard was hungry for more – 'real wealth, fame, and power, the three components of my American Dream'. It was here the Williams' tennis story began. Richard recalls how he decided to have more children and pursue tennis success with them.

> One Sunday, we were all watching television and I asked Yetunde to change the channels. We didn't have a remote, so she patiently turned from one channel to the next and waited for my approval. As programs flashed across the screen, something caught my attention... I will never forget standing there in amazement, watching the tournament director present a twenty-five-year-old professional tennis player from Romania named Virginia Ruzici a forty-thousand-dollar check for winning the tournament. Announcer Bud Collin's next words rang in my ears "That's not bad for four days work".

Richard couldn't believe anyone could earn money that quickly. He went to the store and bought a newspaper the next day to confirm the results. When it turned out to be true, he said to himself, 'I'm going to have two kids and put them into tennis.'[6] Richard remembers his excitement at the potential opportunities:

> I raced home and went into my office and

read the article over and over again. I found myself fantasising about my as-yet-unborn daughters playing tennis. If one woman could win that much money, I wanted *two* daughters to play the game. Double the winnings! After that, I sat in my office thinking and planning everything I'd have to do to succeed. The more I thought about it, the more realistic the idea became.[7]

After the lightning bolt of an idea to have another two girls and help them become tennis superstars, Richard's life took on a completely new meaning: building the best possible environment for tennis success. He had lofty ambitions for his daughters, wanting them to be remembered not because they were 'African Americans' but 'distinguished because they are going to dominate the game'. To do this, he needed to start a new trend in tennis: players who were 'bigger, better, faster, taller', starting with his soon-to-be daughters. There was a small hurdle in their way; neither Richard nor Oracene knew how to play tennis, let alone teach it to their kids (the only option given their income). Richard duly bought some instructional books and videos and taught himself the game.

He took what he liked from coaches around him, being receptive to different techniques and philosophies. The result of his studying was the development of an 'open stance' that he would learn himself and subsequently teach his kids. Instead of standing with feet facing to the side of the court when playing a shot, as was traditional, feet would be facing towards the opponent, allowing for more power generation in the strokes. It would prove to be revolutionary. However, like many radical ideas, at the clubs he practised at around Long Beach he was laughed at his unconventional way of playing. Once he started to gain some success with this technique against these very same club players, he went on to teach Oracene while she was pregnant with Venus. Both were athletic and developed quickly enough that, by the time Venus and Serena were born, they could make a pretty good go at trying to teach them.

It wasn't just tennis practice that Richard was doing to prepare for the arrival of his daughters. He created a detailed 78-page manual for both before they were born, highlighting every step that they needed to become professional players. His attention to detail was staggering.

The often-told story of the Williams sisters is that, growing up in Compton, one of the worst neighbourhoods in the United States, they managed to climb out of the ghetto to superstardom in tennis. They are the classic rags-to-riches story, held up as poster girls of the American Dream. The actual story reveals something even more interesting about their father and the extent of his dedication to making them champions.

As has been mentioned earlier, following the success of Richard's security business in Compton, the family had moved out and were living in a nice house in Long Beach. The whole family were settled, happy with the short walk to the beach. However, Richard's manual included a specific location for Venus and Serena's upbringing:

> What led me to Compton was my belief that the greatest champions came out of the ghetto. I had studied sports successes like Muhammad Ali, and great thinkers like Malcolm X. I saw where they came from. As part of the plan, I decided it was where the

girls were going to grow up, too. It would make them tough, give them a fighter's mentality. They'd be used to combat. And how much easier would it be to play in front of thousands of white people if they had already learned to play in front of score of armed gang members?[8]

Rather than being forced to live in Compton, Richard recalls that the move was a *decision* made by himself for the purposes of their sporting development – even given the certain detrimental impact it would have on other aspects of their life.

This breath-taking logic was something that even his wife, Oracene, raged against. She did not want to give up their house in Long Beach to move to dangerous Compton. But there were other reasons for the move, aside from toughening up the kids' mentality; rent would go down from over $1,000 a month to $135, meaning he could work less and coach more. Also, the nearby public tennis courts were rarely used for tennis; if he could wrestle them back from the gangs, he would have unlimited practice time. This would prove a vital tool in their development. Richard understood a fundamental factor related to practice – he needed to secure maximum practice time in order for the girls to improve. This meant ensuring he had to work as little as possible and have the right facilities available. Bizarrely, his decision to move to Compton actually created a better environment for developing the children as athletes.

Eventually, Oracene was convinced to move to Compton, against her better judgement. Her fears were well founded once they moved in. Richard had severely underestimated the extent that gangs and violence had overtaken Compton and made it an almost impossible place to live. The sounds of gunshots and people dying were a regular occurrence, and it was only that the girls were so young that they didn't notice how dangerous the environment was around them. Richard himself called it 'a living hell'. He would go out every day to try and get the courts back from the many drug dealers who used the spot. He was beaten up many times when trying to wrestle back control of the courts.

Serena and Venus' childhoods contain numerous stories of their father's counter-intuitive logic towards providing the 'best facilities' for practice. Whereas many believed they used old, beaten-up tennis balls due to a lack of money, in his autobiography Richard writes that a primary reason for using them was to build the ability to hit the ball hard, so they would reap the benefits of hitting new balls later on. Instead of giving his girls the best possible facilities during training, he often gave them sub-standard equipment at the beginning to develop their skills even further – and make the game relatively easy when they reached the pristine courts and new balls of the elite game.

Direct comparison can be drawn between this and Futsal, the version of football that is played primarily in Brazil. In this version, a smaller, heavier ball is used, 'a ball that could not be lofted into the air, but demands speed of mind, fleetness of foot, flair and flamboyance',[9] along with small pitches and goals. This develops close control, technique and skill that, when played at a junior level, makes regular football comparatively easy. Futsal, which has become a worldwide phenomenon, has produced many of the greatest players ever to grace the game: Ronaldinho, Pele, Lionel Messi, Cristiano Ronaldo and Neymar[10] all played during their development. Richard Williams provided the same system in tennis –

fluffed up, old tennis balls were harder to hit and the courts were uneven, allowing the girls to get used to unusual bounces at a young age.

Primarily under the coaching of Richard on the courts of Compton, the girls progressed quickly according to the plan. He drummed into them the determination, work ethic and commitment required to get to the top. This extended beyond the courts and had a strong self-determinism message. Boards around the house relayed messages such as 'VENUS: YOU MUST TAKE CONTROL OF YOUR FUTURE' and 'SERENA: YOU MUST LEARN TO LISTEN'.

Richard and Oracene focused every aspect of the young girls' lives to improve them as tennis players. As a result of this, discipline was central to Venus and Serena's childhoods. In her autobiography *My Life*,[11] Serena does not shirk the fact that her life was always supremely disciplined in the Williams household:

> My parents were disciplinarians, but on top of that we were taught to be self-disciplined. They were still pretty hard on us, but we were even harder on ourselves. We were expected to do our schoolwork and our chores, and help each other in whatever ways were age-appropriate. We went dutifully to our daily practice sessions, but it wasn't entirely without complaint. His [Richard Williams] schedule was flexible. Our practice sessions? Not as much.[12]

It became clear quickly that they were the best junior tennis players in the state by a long way, beating girls many year groups above them. The lack of competition was beginning to stunt their growth, and the question of elite coaching started to surface in Richard's mind more regularly. The destination for the best in the country was Palm Beach, Florida, attending the Rick Macci Academy. To give them the opportunity to train with the best, the entire family relocated, including moving their older siblings (except for eldest Tunde) in their school years. This was before Serena was 10 years old, and Venus was only a couple of years older than her.

The whole family moved to Haines City, Florida. Serena describes it as a 'backwater place in the middle of the state' where there wasn't much to do, but it offered excellent tennis facilities and the best coaches. Their training increased to 'four to five hours' after school every day, followed by other sports.

It was not long after this sacrifice that Richard began to reap the rewards from the move. Initially, it was Venus who was the hotshot. She turned professional in 1994 at the age of just 14,[13] playing in the 'Bank of the West Classic' in Oakland and going out to the No. 2 seed in the second round. Her skill at such a young age drew widespread mainstream media attention. In 2000, still just 20, she won Wimbledon and the US Open as well as two gold medals at the Olympics in a single year. As of 2017, she has 7 singles majors and 49 career titles to her name.[14]

Eventually, it was Serena who would prove the better player. Serena would power on to an astonishing 23 major titles (to date), the most of any female player in the open era.[15] Her list of records and achievements is long: she has won 72 career titles, holding the position of world No. 1 for 186 consecutive weeks between 2013 and 2016. No other athlete has dominated tennis to the same extent as Serena; many players are beaten by her before she has even taken to the court, such is her fearsome reputation. She is regularly held up as one of the greatest athletes ever across any sport.

As for the prize money? They have surpassed the $40,000 won by Virginia Ruzici by a long way. As of October 2017, Venus has earned $39,900,489 in prize money alone, excluding lucrative sponsorship deals. Serena has earned an even more astonishing $84,463,131. According to Forbes, they have an estimated combined net worth of $245 million.[16,17]

Although Richard Williams' decision to have children to become tennis stars is unusual, it is the execution that is truly mind-boggling. It is one thing to say that you are going to make two kids into female tennis stars, but completely different to actually achieve this. It required unwavering commitment and discipline by Richard in pursuit of this single goal. Coincidentally, this very mindset was exactly what Richard needed to impart on his children if they were going to become champions.

A key part of his training regimen was focused on developing the attitudes in Serena and Venus that were required for success. From the requirement to complete every training session to the cards with messages around the houses, developing the mentality was central to Richard's plan to develop tennis superstars. He sought to teach discipline, determination and work ethic. He believed in this above all else in making the difference to make it to the top – something which supports our understanding of the requirements for the Champion Mindset. He developed the competitiveness and the motivation required for success, whose foundation was these traits.

Are these values something always taught by parents to sporting prodigies? In *Grit*,[18] psychologist Angela

Duckworth's book about success, she describes how the formula for success in any domain can be boiled down to two fundamental factors. The first is that the exemplars of success are 'unusually resilient and hardworking', which she titles 'resilience' and, second, prodigies know 'in a very, very deep way what it was they wanted', which she titles 'passion'. Resilience and passion together make *Grit*, the factor that she has shown best predicts success in everything from cadet training programmes to SAT scores. It also applies to sport.

Central to her theory is that, contrary to popular belief, Grit is not something that we are inherently born with, but something that can be developed. When discussing Parenting for Grit, Duckworth focuses on how setting an example of being gritty as parents can have a significant impact on a child's life in also helping them to become gritty. Furthermore, she also talks about opportunities to develop Grit. A surprising marker of success academically is extracurricular activities – taking positions of responsibility and sticking with an activity for more than one year. This shows the perseverance, determination and discipline to be able to complete hard things that will be transferable to education, particularly when study becomes difficult.

Richard Williams certainly developed gritty children. The reason why he was able to do this so successfully was twofold. First, he was an exemplar of grittiness. He did not hide the hard work he had done and the passion with which he pursued their tennis development. His career had been hard, but he had succeeded despite tough circumstances and persevered in the face of adversity.

Second, he created in his training sessions opportunities to develop their Grit. He always pushed at the limits of what Venus and Serena could do, and this repetitive process of improving helped to improve their grittiness. This focus on one singular goal for a long period of time meets Duckworth's definition of passion too.

Instilling these values of grittiness were a vital component to developing the Champion Mindset. The most competitive children are those willing to persevere in the face of defeat, and still give the required effort to overcome. They also have a clear direction that they follow for years on end. Richard Williams' development of his girls' Grit was a core component in developing their Champion Mindset.

Many parents of champions, in a similar way to Richard, stressed the importance of living a disciplined life that was characterised by commitment and a strong work ethic, developing Grit that would help in competition. But on the surface, an anomaly to this requirement is Usain Bolt. His attitude is the Jamaican ideal of a laid-back lifestyle. At any race, from a local meet to international finals, he can always be seen relaxing until the very last moment on the track by gesturing to the crowd while laughing and joking with his competitors; not to their amusement.

But behind the joyful exterior, there is a real steel to Bolt's character. He grew up in the small village of Sherwood Content in Trelawny Parish, Jamaica. Usain grew up with an irrepressible energy that made him a mischievous child. He was always up to something when out playing with the other kids on the dusty roads surrounding their simple house. But Bolt's parents were not going to let him grow up naughty.

'[You] can't hope to take gold medals or break world records without discipline. And boy, there was some hard work and discipline in the Bolt home – *serious discipline*' recalls Usain in his autobiography, *Faster than Lightning*.[19] Wellesley Bolt, a strict traditional father, saw discipline as one of his absolute requirements to teach his children.

He required total respect and politeness towards everyone. As a young child aged five on his way to Waldensia Primary School, Bolt had to say hello to everyone he passed – without fail. A tiny Bolt, walking early in the morning, would dutifully say hello to every individual, often well over 20 people. If he didn't, Bolt's father would find out and there would be consequences. It shows the strictness with which Bolt's father implemented his rules, whether large or small.

When Bolt finished primary school, he received a scholarship to William Knibb High School due to his sprinting potential. His father would wake Bolt up at 5.30 a.m. because he didn't 'believe in lateness to school'. Once he was at school, he was not entirely free of the gaze of his father. He ensured he continued to conduct himself with the upmost discipline in all of his activities. 'I always would go to William Knibb once per week to see him train,' said Wellesley. 'In the early part he would try to skip training sometimes to go and play those video games in Falmouth. I always had to be on top of that.'[20]

Although Bolt admits some of his father's techniques to implement discipline are frowned upon now, he is entirely sure that the discipline he learned made him into the man he is today. Bolt closely links his work ethic to the influence of his parents too; constantly being branded as lazy had a deep effect on his work ethic:

> There were chores to do for the family, even as a kid and, oh man, did I have to work

sometimes! Pops was worried that I wouldn't pick up the same work ethic that he had when he was little, so once I'd got old enough he would always tell me to do the easier jobs around the house, like the sweeping. Most of the time I was cool with it, but if ever I ran off, he would start complaining. 'Oh, the boy is lazy', said Dad, time after time. 'He should do some more work around the place'.[21]

As Bolt grew older, he was handed a major task; collecting water. The family did not have piped water, and therefore Bolt needed to take a bucket to the river before pouring the water into tanks in their family yard, usually having to make 48 trips to complete the daily task. He became so sick of it he forced himself to carry two at once, halving the number of trips and having the unintended consequence of building his strength. This kind of manual labour began to develop him physically, but more importantly developed a discipline and work ethic that would pay dividends in getting the most out of training sessions – even when he hated it.

But it was not just the chores and rules that helped to develop the mentality of a young Bolt; the example set by his parents was also a significant influencer. Wellesley was a manager at a coffee company and would be required to work long hours right across Jamaica to visit various plantations. Most nights he returned late and, in Bolt's own words, was always 'working, working, working' from when Bolt was very young.

After being made redundant by the coffee company, Bolt's father set up a small convenience shop in Sherwood Content. He still runs it to this day. This need to continue working, even when his son is making enough money for him never to have to lift a finger again, demonstrates his work ethic.

It wasn't just his father who had this drive. His mother Jennifer Bolt, a dressmaker, would always be working at home repairing clothes. She was known as the best in the village and would work relentlessly hard. Once Bolt became a little older, he was required to help, once again teaching him the value of work.

Surrounded by two parents who worked incredibly hard themselves, Usain internalised that this was required for success. He calls it out as being the most important part of his childhood in shaping his future.

Again, we can see that Usain Bolt's parents developed the mental attributes in him in the same two ways as Richard Williams. They developed grit both through being examples and providing opportunities. Usain's mother and father exemplified the mental attributes they sought to pass on to Usain due to their hard work and discipline in their own lives. They also used chores, such as sweeping and collecting water, to ensure Usain developed the discipline and perseverance needed for success.

Although there are similarities in terms of developing the mental attributes required for success, their level of sacrifice to promote sporting opportunities is radically different. The Williams' parents gave up practically everything in pursuit of the tennis dream. However, in the case of Usain Bolt, his parents did not have to make nearly the same sacrifices. They were able to maintain their lives in Sherwood Content, and still live there today in a not too dissimilar fashion to when Usain was born (albeit with a few upgrades since Usain's success). So why did this differ so radically from the experience of the Williams' parents?

Usain's opportunity to sprint at an elite level was presented through the school system and Jamaican athletics association.

Other groups took the strain of organisation and support. In Compton, no one even played tennis – there were few opportunities for organised training, and therefore Richard and Oracene Williams had to step in. In nearly all cases, parents will have to make some commitment of time and money, but the extent to which this sacrifice is required is related to the local infrastructure in place to support individuals in developing that sport. The more support, the less parental sacrifice needs to be made. We'll look at these other supporting factors for success later in this book.

What is universal is that when parents saw that a child had a passion for a sport, they actively encouraged it and did everything possible to create more opportunities for them. Ensuring they had the best opportunities is vital to being able to climb the ladder to become one of the best.

However, it is not just about the creation of opportunities and mentality. Perhaps one of the most famous parents of a champion is Earl Woods, Tiger's father. His book *Training a Tiger*[22] describes his experiences of bringing up a golf prodigy. Earl Woods himself was a former US Army infantry officer who served two tours of duty in Vietnam and retired with the rank of lieutenant colonel. He had always wanted to be a sports star, and when he became a parent he decided to throw everything at helping his child reach that goal instead.

Before he could even walk, Earl would place Tiger in a baby chair in the garage behind him while he practised his strokes. He hoped this would help to encode the movements in his young mind. When he was old enough to play, Earl was able to train Tiger through his early childhood years. He instilled an army-like discipline to the completion of drills and training and would create an environment of striving for perfection that Tiger became totally obsessed with, even after his father passed away. He would implore his dad every night to take him to the course and would always want more time practising.

The reason that Tiger could not wait to get back out on the greens was because of the relationship he had with father. He adored him and couldn't wait for him to return home from work. Given the mental strain required to improve at golf, having someone that is supportive of you, and positively encourages you in your endeavours, is critical.

Earl Woods speaks specifically in *Training A Tiger* of this need to be a supporter and a friend to Tiger, rather than simply a coach who barked out instructions. Although he was widely considered a father who had a disciplined nature, he was also able to provide the support needed to a young Tiger rising through the ranks. He talks of how 'You can never say to a child too often that I love you', and that you need to 'laugh and cry with your child'.[23] These comments contrast with the stereotypical father role of being masculine and not emotionally connected – Earl Woods suggests this is critical to success.

ESPN writer Wright Thompson recounts Tiger and his dad's relationship:

> Tiger and Earl did everything together, hitting balls into a net out in the garage, or spending hours at the golf course, and when they'd finish, Earl would order a rum and

Diet Coke, and Tiger would get a Coke with cherries, and they'd sit and nurse their drinks like two old men. The golf pro at the Navy course, Joe Grohman, worried that Tiger didn't have friends his own age until high school. His friends were Earl and Earl's old military buddies.[24]

They were so close, that when Earl passed away in 2006, Tiger's life quickly spiralled out of control. For all the parents of these champions, the relationship with their child was of the utmost importance. Nearly all of those studied had an extremely close and loving relationship with their parents, who were a pillar in their lives to help guide them and be a friend as well as a parent. The reality is that most of the children involved in elite sport are working so hard that mainly they attend school, train and don't have time to do much else. Therefore, most of their friends often come from the sport, and the relationship with parents often becomes even more important in their life.

However, issues begin to emerge when parents need to teach discipline and work ethic to create the attributes for athletic success. Discipline can be associated with a more authoritarian method of parenting, which could potentially have a damaging effect on the relationship. It's a delicate balancing act between both being a supporter and remaining that parent figure who can impose discipline.

So, what have we learned about parents? Unsurprisingly, they play an absolutely vital role in the lives of children who go on to become champions. First, all parents play an important role in helping to develop the mental attributes for success – in particular, the grittiness that ensures that a Champion Mindset of competitiveness and motivation is sustained over the long term. This can be done either through a parent's involvement in sport, or more general activities growing up. Second, parents can be important in determining that there are opportunities to progress in sport for young prodigies. This often requires a level of sacrifice that is inversely related to the external support for a sport. Finally, the relationship with the child is of upmost importance. As a bedrock in these children's lives, a good relationship can ensure the sporting journey remains positive, despite its inherent difficulties.

5

Siblings

It's the final race of the 2016 men's triathlon world series in Cozumel, Mexico.[1] Jonny Brownlee is bidding to win his first world championship and leads the race by a distance entering the closing stages. To clinch the title, he needs to finish in first position and arch rival, Spaniard Mario Mola, to finish no higher than fourth. Jonny seems a certainty for victory, but with just a few metres to go things start to go badly wrong. In perfect control up to this point, he starts lurching towards the barriers. In the sweltering Mexican heat, he has become dehydrated to the point of exhaustion. Legs flailing like a seasick sailor, he stumbles towards the hoardings as he desperately tries to will himself forwards, to victory.

Brother Alistair, in second position, quickly approaches him and hardly flinches in racing over to help his younger sibling. He flings Jonny's limp arm over his shoulders and begins to run him to the finish. Schoeman, a South African athlete, passes into the lead, but Brownlee can still potentially win the title. Jonny, with the support of Alistair, is now running with his head flung back in a way that no one in control of their body would. He is edging ever closer to the finish with his brother's help, the line agonisingly close. Both Alistair and Jonny throw feverish glances back, looking for other competitors in the field. Jonny manages one final effort, swinging his free arm to get more traction. Just as he seems to be certain to make it, he falters. It is only a push from Alistair that helps him to collapse over the line in second, totally exhausted.

Footage of the spectacle of the big brother carrying his little brother across the finish line in a world triathlon race went viral. Mola's fifth position in the race denied Jonny the title, but those dramatic scenes brought more adulation to the Brownlees than a win ever would have done. The admiration for their brotherly compassion was acknowledged far and wide. But Alistair had some typical words for his younger brother afterwards: 'I wish the flipping idiot had just paced it right and won the race.'[2]

The stories of brothers Alistair and Jonathan Brownlee have always been inextricably linked. They have dominated the triathlon scene since 2009 and remain to this day the best triathletes in the world. Alistair won the gold medal in the Olympics in 2012 and 2016, with Jonny collecting a bronze and a silver respectively. They are a phenomenon within the sport. It's astonishing that the two best triathletes in the world, in such a hyper-competitive sport, are from the same family.

Both Alistair and Jonny recall spending much of their childhood outdoors on adventures, with the local Yorkshire Dales their playground.[3] On visits to the family house on the moors, they would push their physical boundaries on long days out together, heading off miles from home with no form of communication, completely independent. They would swim and sail in the lake behind the house, and cycle or run along the narrow winding roads across the fells.

When they were old enough to enter competitions, the moors remained a focal point. They regularly entered fell-running races, an eccentric sport that involves running off-road on the moors across highly undulating routes. It was one of the defining features of the Brownlees' childhoods.

From an early age, Alistair revelled in the three triathlon disciplines of swimming, cycling and running. Regardless of weather, he would head out in a vest and shorts for a run; nothing could stop him. Despite starting out as one of the worst athletes in school, finishing lowly in early school Cross country races, his progress was fast. He quickly showed considerable promise across a range of solo endurance events.

Growing up, Jonny did not get the same inherent enjoyment from triathlon's three disciplines. He much preferred team sports and excelled in the likes of football and cricket. He played football for Leeds United academy and cricket for Yorkshire at a junior level. But once Alistair started bringing home GB kit and medals from triathlons, Jonny fancied getting a piece of the action. Of course, it was easy for him to get involved: he didn't have to work out how to train, but simply tag along with his big brother during his training sessions.

Although brothers, the two could not be more different in terms of personality. Alistair was always independent, strong-willed and had the desire to do it all himself. Jonny hated being on his own. Their dad described Alistair as 'a very self-assured and confident little boy', while he thought Jonny 'worshipped' his big brother.[4] As a small child, Jonny was always looking for Alistair, and felt safe and secure only by his side. When Alistair left for school for the first time, Jonny spent so long crawling around the house looking for him that his knees began to bleed.

It was during their teenage years that the Brownlees accelerated their development as triathletes. Alistair at age 13 was the first to start training seriously with a goal in mind. His first target was to make the Yorkshire representative Cross Country team and, sure enough, met his goal at the first attempt a few months later. So, he set his sights higher. Every new target he set was more ambitious as his confidence grew. He dedicated himself to the target, would put his heart and soul into it, and would invariably succeed. Yorkshire teams became GB teams, and his goals became winning races on the international stage. He reached the pinnacle when he became World Junior Triathlon Champion in 2006 in Lausanne, Switzerland.

When Alistair moved up to the senior ranks following this victory, it finally left room for Jonny to grab the limelight. He excelled at a junior level too but had always been in the background of Alistair's trailblazing success. He had been craving the opportunity to 'make his mark'. Three years after Alistair's victory, Jonny went to the Gold Coast for the World Junior Championships with the real expectation he would win. After building a lead, Mario Mola (winner of the 2016 World Championship mentioned earlier) overtook him, and Jonny couldn't catch up; he would finish in second place. The loss had a real effect on Jonny:

> The mental pain of not winning that race stuck around…. 2009 was supposed to by my big year. Alistair had been champion; I

thought I had to be. To make it worse, Alistair won the senior World Championship that weekend. Again, I felt completely overshadowed. I felt like a failure.[5]

The pressure to live up to his brother had weighed heavily on Jonny – he had just been crowned the second-best junior triathlete in the world, yet still felt like a failure.

But Jonny did not dwell on this negativity for long and did not allow it to crush him. His response, rather than to give up, was to work harder than ever before. In 2010, now in the senior ranks, Jonny doubled down on his training, and was rewarded with success when he came second in the senior ITF World Tour series race in Hyde Park, London. It felt to him like the moment he needed to finally pull out of Alistair's shadow and announce himself as a triathlete.

But again, this monumental moment in Jonny's career was overshadowed by his big brother. In the same Hyde Park race, Alistair collapsed just after the finish line, swaying badly with exhaustion much like Jonny would in Mexico six years later.[6] He was rushed away for medical treatment immediately. After receiving attention from the medical team at the event, he was sent to hospital, where he was later discharged without issue. But the dramatic scenes of the collapse captured the media's attention and was the lead story for many newspapers and websites. Again, the limelight had been taken away from Jonny. The younger brother again persevered, used this as motivation, and wanted even more to prove to everyone that he had a rightful place in elite sport.

While Jonny suffered with the weight of expectation caused by Alistair, the brotherly rivalry was also heaping mental strain on Alistair:

> If you're the older sibling, the pressure to stay ahead is incredible. You have to be very strong to deal with it... No doubt having Jonny biting at my heels my whole life has helped me achieve what I have. There is no bigger motivation you could have, than living with the second-best triathlete in the world.[7]

Their relationship is key to ensuring the Brownlees maintain the motivation they need to train with intensity during every practice session. Traditionally, triathlon is a lonely sport to train in. It requires mostly endurance work, and lots of this is done on your own. The Brownlees have always had each other to compete with. It has propelled both to the top of the world in their sport. If either was to drop out, the resulting change in their training environment would have serious consequences for the other's quality of training and performance.

Like the Brownlees, the success of the Williams sisters will always be associated with each other. Their father, Richard, prepared his manual to develop his two future tennis superstars and moved the family to Compton in pursuit of the best environment for his girls to become professional tennis players.[8] Developing two girls in tennis, similar in age, led to inevitable comparisons being drawn between the two.

For Serena, no figure was as important in her life as her sister, Venus. She worshipped her older sibling, and simply wanted to be her: 'She cast a big shadow, I'll say that. She was taller, prettier, quicker, more athletic. And, she was certainly *nicer*. There was no living up to her. I certainly tried. I wanted to do everything just like Venus.'[9]

Her total admiration for her sister was tinged with frustration at feeling like she was constantly in her shadow. As the hype around Venus grew, Serena felt like she was clinging to the coattails of her big sister: 'When we were little it was always "Venus this" and "Venus that." "Venus, Venus, Venus." The more we developed as players, the more I became the tagalong kid sister. That was the perception.'

Despite her parents' constant support, Serena's confidence was knocked by the comparisons:

> Growing up on those tennis courts in Compton and Lynwood and all over Los Angeles, it sometimes felt like nobody believed in me. I suppose I understand it on some level. Clearly, Venus was the phenom, the prodigy, the rising star.
> But on another level, it hurt. Even my dad, who's always been my biggest supporter, was spending more time with Venus, more time on her game, more time talking to reporters and coaches about her.[10]

In fact, when Serena became demoralised, it was her relationship with Venus that kept her strong and ensured she remained motivated. Venus was always there to offer support to her kid sister, and the two were inseparable. Her kind-hearted nature did wonders to ensure that Serena did not become too demoralised with the situation. Venus would constantly tell her that her 'time would come' and to 'stay positive', helping Serena in her darker moments.

By the time Venus had reached nine years old, the gap in standard between her and Serena was growing rather than shrinking. Serena had not developed physically, describing herself as the 'runt-of-the-litter,' while Venus was well developed at an early age, standing tall and strong. The lack of competition for Venus within the family led to their dad relenting from his laser-like focus on training and allowed Venus to enter tournaments – but only if she could beat him in a competitive match. Sure enough, she beat him that year, and began entering tournaments across the United States. Serena was happy for her sister, but with the whole family having to travel in tow to these events, she resented that the focus had shifted even more to her sister.

Serena badly wanted to be involved in tournaments and prove her worth. Every day she would ask her father to be allowed just one opportunity. But he wouldn't let her, wanting her to practise more instead. The frustration at not being able to show her potential grew until, one day, she got the opportunity – albeit not by design from her father.

Serena noticed that her dad had brought home two application forms for an upcoming tournament. Serena filled one in secretly and sent it off without the entry fee (as she had no money with which to pay). She crossed her fingers and desperately hoped that the organisers would accept it and enter her in the competition.

Serena would usually take her kit to Venus' tournaments anyway, so that she could hit some balls with her parents during breaks. No one thought it unusual when she arrived at this tournament ready to play. But for Serena, nerves jangling, this was a huge moment in her young life. She went to the desk, found out her opponent and court number, and snuck off to her first ever competitive match. After finding out, her father was shocked – but supportive. He seemed to be amused by Serena's deviance and desire to compete. She won her first game, and immediately afterwards she began planning with her father how to beat her next opponent.

By chance, the sisters had been put in opposite sides of the draw, and both played well to make it all the way to the final. Venus won easily, as Serena expected. Overall, the family returned from the tournament happy with their day's work - except for Serena. Her silver trophy felt like nothing compared to Venus' gold one, such was her fierce competitiveness. After making obvious her frustration at not getting the gold one, in an act of sisterly love, Venus gave her the gold trophy. It was a moment of kindness that Serena was a little overcome by. She still has it to this day.

The comparisons continued as the girls accumulated junior tournaments, particularly from the media who grew fascinated with the two girls from Compton who were playing tennis from a different planet. Serena vividly remembers a national newspaper article when they had just started playing in competitions. It said that she would 'never be more than a footnote to Venus's career'.[11] Serena never forgot that article. She promised she would prove that reporter wrong and used it to fuel her motivation.

Proving the comparisons wrong remains a powerful motivator for Serena, but she is well aware of the effect her older sister had on her career – she even questions if she would have made it to the top without Venus:

> Throughout my development, there was always Venus to set the standard. At times, when I was little, it seemed like an impossible standard, but there it was. She was the embodiment of my best self. She was the player I wanted to be – the *person* I wanted to

99

be, too.

Really, I don't know where I would get that drive, were it not for Venus. I suppose I would have found it somewhere, but it might have taken awhile.[12]

Now, it feels like the roles may have changed a little. Venus recently described her seven majors as 'chump change' in comparison to Serena's record-breaking 23. She said about her little sister getting engaged: 'She's much smarter than I am, she's a wise woman. She's actually getting a real life. She's paving the way, once again, for me. Maybe I'll grow up.'[13]

In both the cases of the Brownlee brothers and the Williams sisters, their relationship to each other was a defining element of their childhood. The siblings were close in age and competed against each other almost on a daily basis, leading to both developing faster than if they were progressing individually. This competition against each other played a crucial role in creating the environment to foster the Champion Mindset. The raw competitiveness was honed by being engaged with it every single day in training sessions together. As anyone who has trained in a group will know, it is also much easier to maintain motivation when working alongside someone of a similar level. Both the competitiveness and motivation factors in the Champion Mindset were influenced for the Williams sisters and Brownlee brothers by being siblings.

In the end, it was the older Brownlee brother and younger Williams sister who proved more successful. On a wider scale, how does having siblings affect your sporting development? In 2010, three universities collaborated on the Pathways to the Podium project[14] – a multisport, multinational investigation of the development of sport expertise. The project aimed to gain an understanding of the pathways that athletes follow on their way towards attaining peak performance. As part of the project, they looked at the influence of siblings on sporting success.

In a study of 229 athletes, it found that 'elite athletes were more likely to be later-born children, while pre-elite and non-elite athletes were more likely to be first-born'.[15] It also studied the influence siblings have on the likelihood of playing elite sport. If an older sibling was playing elite sport, the younger sibling was four times more likely to be competing in elite sport compared to the control group. Older siblings were more than twice as likely to take part in any sport if younger siblings were involved in elite sport.

This reveals two important discoveries. Firstly, younger siblings tend to be more successful. Why this is the case remains unknown but, taking the case of Venus and Serena Williams, we can suggest a couple of potential reasons why. First, Serena always had the benchmark of Venus playing at a higher level. This ensured Serena was constantly pushing herself to match her level of performance, even though she was younger. Venus did not have this luxury and was instead breaking barriers herself. Second, Serena had the benefit of her father's experience of training Venus from a young age. Although he had a carefully detailed plan for both, he would have learned things from training Venus that he could apply to the training of Serena, helping her progress more efficiently when she first started playing. This could help to explain why younger siblings tend to be more successful elite athletes.

Secondly, younger siblings are more likely to compete at an elite level if their older sibling is already competing in elite sport. Here, we seem to be seeing the impact of a 'follow me' effect – following the path and example set by the older brother or sister is easier than starting from scratch in a new sport with no one to follow or guide you. Therefore, success is more likely when an older sibling plays the sport. It's much harder to follow a younger sibling as an older sibling; you are at a disadvantage in terms of sporting development and age. This study does help to show why we see many more siblings in elite sport than we would expect statistically.

But given the benefits of having siblings on sporting performance, why is it that there are not more siblings competing in the same sport together at the elite level? Alistair Brownlee alluded to this earlier in the chapter whilst describing his relationship with Jonny. The intensity of always being in competition with your brother or sister is huge and takes a big mental toll. It's hard to have to complete to be the best in your family at something. Often, this leads siblings to pursue other avenues so as not to be directly compared to their siblings, and as such we see children striking out in completely different directions from each other. Although it is beneficial in a development capacity to compete in the same sport, the inevitable tensions make it extremely difficult to do so.

Sibling rivalry plays a role in many of our sporting champions' childhoods. Although unusual for both to make it to elite sport, the likes of Michael Jordan, Paula Radcliffe, Michael Phelps, Sachin Tendulkar and Andy Murray all had siblings who played their sport to a good level and were important to their development. It can be an important factor in creating the right environment to develop the Champion Mindset.

6
School

For us all, school is perhaps the single most defining element of our childhood, providing the structure around which daily life is built. Due to the sheer amount of time we spend at school, it inevitably plays a significant role in all aspects of our development – including sport. The story is no different for our champions. For some, it offered great opportunities for sporting progression through coaching, facilities and competition whilst for others it was a constant thorn in their side that got in the way of what they really wanted to do.

The link between school and sporting success can vary widely and is dependent on a few key factors. The most important factor is the popularity of the sport within your home country. The more popular the sport, the more likely schools will play an active role in your development. American Football is perhaps the best example of a sport integrated with the education system. It forms a major focus of many US education institutions, where star players are revered by fellow students and matches provide a focal point for the whole school.

Practically the only way to progress in the sport is through the school system; coaching, practice and games are all embedded within the school routine.

More specialist sports have a much more distant relationship with school. Those that require specific equipment, such as kayaking or rowing, get barely any coverage at all on the standard school programme. At best, school can provide welcome financial relief to help those access sport, or time to go and engage in high quality practice, but the two will never have a link like American Football does with US colleges.

When we looked at the upbringing of the Brownlee brothers in the last chapter, it was clear that their teenage years represented an important formative period. For all their wild adventures, it was their high school, Bradford Grammar, that would prove the centrepiece to their development. The brothers remember how Bradford Grammar had a 'sporting culture that could not have been more conducive to our development'.[1] Tony Kingham was the coach of the cross-country team at the school. Usually derided by students at most schools, at Bradford Grammar cross-country running was popular, often with 50 heading to the Saturday races organised by the school, and weekday runs being equally well attended. This provided the platform for competition that developed the Brownlees' love of running.

But perhaps more important than the opportunity to run was the culture. With such a focus on sport, the Brownlees were allowed to disappear off at lunchtimes on runs – which always seemed better to the teenage boys than staying in school. They would head out nearly every midday to Lister Park or the woods around Bradford for a range of workouts. Particularly important were the long runs on Wednesdays, when the school left afternoons free for sport.

This gave them an opportunity to train an additional five hours each week. The Brownlees were given total freedom to go off and do whatever they wanted. Other students may not have seized such an opportunity, but the Brownlees relished the chance to go out and run. Their love for the outdoors and physical activity meant they took the opportunity to improve. Mostly. Alistair admits to getting fish and chips every Friday and doing his fair amount of messing around in the woods alongside his running. Jonny remembers the kudos of running at lunchtime: 'The best thing about going running at lunchtime? You were allowed to go the front of the lunch queue. Priceless.'[2]

There were extra little steps that helped to further Jonny and Alistair Brownlee's training. For example, in sixth form, Alistair was given special treatment for his attendance. It didn't matter if he attended registrations, as long as he completed his schoolwork and went to lessons. As Alistair himself puts it, the school attitude was 'if I was running, I was running. It didn't matter'.[3]

The school's leniency meant that, in a busy and packed school day, it helped the Brownlees get the time they needed to train. By developing a culture that rewarded cross-country running, Alistair and Jonny Brownlee trained like never before and had a supportive environment that helped them develop their abilities.

Running would become the key weapon of both the Brownlee brothers: whilst they were just world-class in swimming and cycling, they could decimate the field during the run to clinch their world and Olympic titles. The rest of the field would fear the kicks that would come at the end of the triathlon, often in partnership. This was in no small amount down to Tony Kingham and Bradford Grammar High School.

The Brownlees were supported in their quest to become great by their school, but much of their training took place externally. There are other examples amongst the champions where school played a more fundamental role in athletic success, driving the coaching, practice and competition. One particular example stands out from the rest: how a school developed the cricket great Sachin Tendulkar, almost single-handedly.

Sachin Tendulkar was born in Bombay in 1973, the youngest of four siblings. It was his half-brother, Ajit, who introduced him to the game. Growing up in Mumbai, Sachin was regarded as a bully and was not averse to picking a fight or two.[4] He particularly enjoyed tennis, and his idol was John McEnroe due to the bursts of temper he would show on the court. At the same time Sachin was also playing cricket with friends, and he would play both with Ajit together at home.[5]

Eventually, Ajit took him to a trial to join a highly competitive summer camp run by prominent local coach, Ramakant Achrekar. It was an opportunity to get some world-class training, as Ramakant Achrekar had coached a number of players for the Indian national team. In that trial, Sachin played poorly due to nerves. It was only because his older brother managed to convince Ramakant to take another look at him that he got a second trial, which was much more successful. He spent the summer dutifully improving his batting technique at the camp.

Afterwards, he was encouraged by Ramakant to join Shardashram Vidyamandir school, where he was coach, to further develop his cricket abilities. In local cricket circles, this was known as a great school for developing talent. In comparison, his current school, the New English School in Bandra, had very few cricket facilities.

This was no small decision for the young Sachin. The school was an hour and a half away and would take even longer if he missed his connecting bus. He also had the social impacts of changing schools at the age of 11: 'The move meant I lost contact with a lot of my New English School friends, but I soon made new ones at Shardashram, mostly through cricket.'[6] The sport proved to be the common interest that bound him and his new classmates together.

Once at Shardashram school, cricket quickly became Sachin's world. The school was devoted to developing the next generation of cricket stars. When he joined, Tendulkar was surrounded by many other high-quality junior cricketers, many who made it to a professional standard and even played for India with him. This competition instantly reset Tendulkar's expectations of himself to a higher level of performance. The school also offered the chance to use better-quality cricket equipment for the first time. The introduction of nets allowed Tendulkar to face many more balls in a standard practice, and therefore accelerate his development.

Finally, and most importantly, Tendulkar had the full-time coaching of Ramakant Achrekar, who was no stranger to developing elite players. A number of Indian internationals had already developed under his tutelage during their childhoods.[7] Ramakant took Tendulkar under his wing and did everything he could to develop him.

When he began playing for the school's team, he

scored massive totals in epic batting displays that belied his age. In his trailblazing season that is still talked about in India, at the age of 14, he made a century in every single innings that he played. At the tender age of just 15, he made his first-class debut for Bombay, before appearing for India a year later.

It all appears to have been worthwhile – Tendulkar is revered as one of the greatest batsmen in history. His crowning glory is his record as the only man ever to score 100 test centuries in international cricket. He scored a staggering 15,291 runs in his 200 tests with an average of 53.78. He went on to help India win the Cricket World Cup in 2011, an equally accomplished player in the 50-over version of the game. He was the only Indian player to be named in *Wisden Cricketers' Almanack* all-time World Test XI in 2013.[8]

Tendulkar's turning point in his young career was when he moved schools. Following the summer camp – which he scraped into thanks to his brother – the opportunity to improve came about as a result of attending a new school. Sachin himself considers joining the new school as vital to his development:

> Joining Shardashram undoubtedly helped my cricket a great deal. It allowed me the opportunity to play competitive matches regularly and my game rapidly improved as a result.[9]

In particular, Sachin recognises the importance of having access to coach Achrekar at the school in his ascension to professional cricket:

> Looking back at these years of cricket, I must say I owe a lot to my coach Ramakant Achrekar – as well as his assistants, Das

Shivalkar and Laxman Chavan. Had it not been for Sir, I would not be the cricketer I turned out be. He was a strict disciplinarian and did everything he could for me...On certain days he would drive me all the way across Mumbai on his scooter to get me to matches on time.[10]

All of these opportunities were made available by the school, affording Sachin prospects he simply could never have accessed through private means. Equality of opportunity is a core tenet of schools in general, and in sport it can play a pivotal role. Of course, it required Tendulkar to have the mentality and the talent to be able to seize these opportunities and improve at an exceptional rate. But Shardashram Vidyamandir school gave him the opportunity to flourish and, as such, was the enabler of his success.

In the examples of the Brownlees and Tendulkar, their schools had very strong cultures around the sports that our champions were pursuing. Cricket and cross-country running are common sports in Indian and British schools respectively. Cricket is a religion in India; a close affinity between sport and country which is practically unparalleled anywhere in the world. Similarly, Britain has a rich history of school cross-country running, albeit the sport is not loved as widely as cricket in India. Forced upon many a shivering, fed up high-school student, running laps round a muddy field is still a rite of passage although, for the majority, interaction with the sport ends there.

Therefore, with it ingrained in school life, it was likely the education system would play a key role in the development of Tendulkar and the Brownlees. When physical education lessons were being planned out by teachers, these sports were at the forefront of their minds, as they have featured in school programmes in these countries for generations. Schools were likely to contribute to these sporting career paths. However, the difference between Bradford Grammar and Shardashram Vidyamandir and other schools is the extent to which sporting culture dominated the school and the sacrifices they were willing to make for improvement. PE coaches were skilled and deeply passionate about developing their athletes, going above and beyond what is normally expected from a teacher. Schools were proud of the achievements of their students, and actively encouraged sporting development.

The relationship between school and sporting ambitions is not always as well aligned as this. In the case of Michael Phelps, we can see the other side of how school can affect sporting development.

Michael Phelps spent most of his free time as a kid at the Meadowbrook Aquatics and Fitness Center, training in the pool.[11] These facilities weren't available at his place of education, Towson High School. Instead, school proved to be a real pain point for a young Phelps. In lessons, he struggled to concentrate and stay focused and did not fit in particularly well with his classmates. He was diagnosed with ADHD in sixth grade and took a course of Ritalin for several years. Although knowing how important it was, for Phelps, school was more of a chore than a place to really foster his sporting talent. It proved a test of his mettle to stay with it, particularly while having to juggle it with his extreme training regime.

When Bob Bowman told Michael and his mum that he could make the Olympics, he had a specific set of requirements that would need to be followed. One was that Phelps needed to work hard in the pool. Another was that Phelps needed school to better understand his swimming requirements and be more accommodating in helping studies fit around his intense training schedule:

> My academic track in high school had to be designed, with help from teachers and school administrators, to allow me to fulfil the essential Maryland state requirements for a diploma but no more. No honours classes, no advanced placement. Could it be worked out so that I might on some days be allowed to arrive at school later than other kids? Might it be possible to be let out early?[12]

The very nature of Phelps' sport meant that school was going to play a different role in his childhood as he strove for sporting success; it needed to be a facilitator rather than an active developer.

School can present a wonderful opportunity to access high-quality facilities and coaches. As was the case with Sachin Tendulkar, there are many high-quality coaches in the education system who have a deep passion for their chosen sports and are willing to go above and beyond to help children fulfil their potential. This often removes the financial barrier that can be so prohibitive to accessing high-quality coaches through other means. For those for whom sport is readily available in school, only their commitment is a barrier to the extent to which they can improve, regardless of level of talent.

Of course, teaching sport at school in general has a more holistic focus to get every child active. Being engaged in sport can have numerous benefits – developing social skills, a success mindset, time management, a healthy lifestyle and even contributing towards better academic success.[13] Sport still plays a crucial role socially in schools and can build friendships and bonds that define school times for many children. This is important and shouldn't be overlooked in pursuit of elite sport achievement. The need to develop good habits and a positive relationship with an active lifestyle will remain at the core of the focus for school physical education departments.

However, becoming an elite athlete requires schools to go the extra mile, either by being especially lenient or providing exceptional opportunities. Particularly during teenage years, where individuals are transitioning to the senior ranges, elite sports training is something that rarely can be fitted around other focuses – academic or otherwise. Therefore, developing those in the upper echelons of sport requires a completely different mindset that accommodates intense practice for children and that may include helping them with homework, lessons or attendance. If the sport is mainly practised within the school, this makes it easier to combine the two – enhancing the school's reputation helps to smooth this transition to a different focus. But for external pursuits, this can lead to aggravation. Parents play a crucial role in mediating this relationship and ensuring that both goals are met simultaneously.

But offering such leniency does not guarantee a positive outcome. There must be hundreds of thousands of cases where children have stretched to reach the elite level in their sport and have failed due to bad luck or events beyond their control, ending up with very few life prospects due to the spurning of their academic education. We will discuss this in more detail later in this book, but it is important to keep in mind those who do not make it and the potential effect on their lives of a lack of focus on education. This is a trade-off that many children looking to reach the top of their sport must consider but, one way or another, school is a key part of any child's development.

7

Sporting Bodies

A country is often described as a 'factory' when it consistently churns out winners in a particular sport as if from a production line. We've seen the Jamaican Sprint Factory, the Chinese Diving Factory and the British Cycling Factory. It is absolutely remarkable that the most talented athletes in all the world for a single sport could come from the same nation, given the intensity of international competition.

Understanding why this happens is complicated and whole books such as Richard Moore's *The Bolt Supremacy: Inside Jamaica's Sprint Factory*[1] have been devoted to understanding why this is the case. Part of the explanation is the influence the sporting body has in providing high-quality practice environments for its most promising athletes – something reflected in the stories of these champions.

Nadia Comăneci stunned the world when, at the age of 14 at the 1976 Montreal Olympics, she scored the first-ever perfect 10. She became an instant icon for young girls around the world following her majestic routine on the uneven bars. What is often forgotten is the astonishing performances that followed during the same Olympics. She would go on to score another six perfect scores in the Games, winning three golds (including the coveted all-around title).[2] In her gymnastics career she would win five Olympic golds, three silvers and a bronze – an impressive haul for a sport in which athletes typically have very short careers.

Nadia's story begins in Onesti, a small town in the east of Romania. Growing up, Nadia was extremely energetic and spent much of her time jumping, climbing and running around the village with friends.[3] The boisterous girl reportedly broke four of her parent's sofas by jumping on them. 'I was a true tomboy, with uncontrollable energy that at times pushed my parents to the limits... I was a wild, strange scrap of a girl.'[4]

To try and rid her of this energy, her mother took her to a gymnastics club called Flame at a local gymnasium. From her very first session, Nadia felt at a home in the gym and loved the challenge of trying to master new moves. One session was quickly followed by another, and it was not long before gymnastics began to overtake all other aspects of her life. She became totally focused on improving herself in the gymnasium. She loved the physicality of the sport and trying out new moves in the fun environment that had been created by her first coach.

Meanwhile, Béla Károlyi, a former national boxing champion and a member of the hammer-throwing team in Romania, had been given permission by the Romanian government to create an 'experimental centralised gymnastic school in Onesti'.[5] When he married his wife, Marta, a member of the Romanian gymnastics team, Béla's attention had been drawn to coaching the sport. His previous sporting experience and connections had helped him get the funding to set up a unit for the development of young female gymnasts.

The atmosphere was intensely competitive. In the 1970s, many communist nations turned to sport as a show of dominance during the Cold War. The Romanians were competing against Bulgaria, Poland and other Eastern Bloc nations in female gymnastics. This competition led the government to provide the resources necessary to create a high-performance training environment.

The gym was to be in Onesti – Nadia's home town. Béla began scouring the area surrounding the town for talent to join his academy. He had little success. After many fruitless searches, Béla was reaching the end of his tether:

> We tested about four thousand children. I went from elementary school to elementary school testing for speed, flexibility, coordination and balance... By the fourth week of testing, we still hadn't found enough kids for the school. And I wasn't satisfied with the physical quality and the natural talent of the girls we had found. I decided to screen for gymnasts one more time.
>
> One day I saw two little blond-headed girls doing cartwheels in the corner of the schoolyard. I approached and watched them very closely – they had something. Brrrring! The school bell rang and the little ones darted inside. Where did they disappear to?
>
> I was ready to give up. It was the end of the day and I had been to every class. I stopped for one last try. "Can anyone do a cartwheel?" I tiredly asked. No answer. I was ready to

walk out when I saw two little blonde heads in the back of the room. "Hey can either of you do a cartwheel?" They whispered to each other and then nodded yes. "Let me see them," I said. Boom, boom – they did perfect cartwheels… I told them to tell their mothers that Béla Károlyi said they could be admitted to Onesti's experimental gymnastics school if they wished.[6]

At the age of seven, Nadia's life changed completely as she began to train full-time to be a gymnast. The centralised training system took care of everything – her accommodation, her food, her training and her education. They gave her facilities and training that a girl from an impoverished town in Romania would not normally have had access to.

Béla and Marta worked on the premise that the children couldn't discipline themselves at that age. As such, they disciplined every aspect of their life. The girls would train four to six hours per day, study for as long as necessary and sleep 8–10 hours. They would also have to eat specific proportions of meat, vegetables and milk, always decided for them.

Nadia's training would be split between spending a few hours a day working with weights, ropes and doing other physical training, and completing gymnastics-specific training. This blend of physical training as well as gymnastics was a result of Béla's belief that strength was as important as skill to develop at that age. Despite the intense training, to Nadia it was always fun. She was far from a standout; she describes herself as quiet, but with a ferocious appetite for work. 'I always wanted to do more than Béla or Marta asked of me – if they said twenty-five push-ups, I'd do fifty. I liked the feeling of improving; I craved accomplishments.'

The coaches demanded a high level of performance. In her first competition, the national championships when Nadia was aged nine, there was a lot riding on the performance of Onesti gym's girls. The government had invested in the programme and wanted to see success. Nadia felt she had something to prove, but the pressure on her coaches Béla and Marta Károlyi was even greater. Nadia fell off the beam twice during her performance. Marta, her coach, was fuming. She was terribly demanding, and only perfection would do.

After that initial failure at the national championships, progress was fast. The girls achieved a silver in the Friendship Cup, a prestigious gymnastics event, before sweeping the board in the European Championships just a year before the Olympics. Nadia won four golds, including the all-around title. She was making rapid progress ahead of the 1976 Montreal Olympics.

But, despite this success at the tender age of 13, Nadia was sheltered from how prodigious a gymnast she was becoming. In the closed world of communist Romania, the usual glory associated with athletic success was not there. Nadia's journey instead was deeply personal, and she craved for more accomplishments and pursuit of success purely for the sake of it rather than any external validation. It was her only path in life, and therefore she devoted herself to it.

The extent to which Nadia's world was in a bubble is astonishing. She arrived at the Olympics believing it was just another competition. She had always been told by her coach and the government that the European Championship was the most important competition in the world. She had never watched the Olympics on television and expected an event like the Friendship Cup.

When she arrived in Montreal, she was totally blown away by the sheer scale of the event:

> What I remember most was that everything – *everything* – was free. You were given a badge, and with it, you could get a soft drink; and you were given matching clothing, bags, hats and pins. To me, it was so high-tech, so strange and exciting and wonderful. That first day, I was afraid to close my eyes because I didn't want to miss anything.

Battling the distraction of the Games is a challenge for all competitors; for 14-year-old Nadia, this was intensified tenfold. Of course, every minute of her day was scheduled, and her food was regulated to be the same as ever – meat and salad. But it was the first time she had seen pizza, cottage cheese, peanut butter or breakfast cereal.

She kept her cool and delivered her precision performances to score six perfect 10s on the way to getting three gold medals (as well as a bronze). To her surprise, on return to Romania she was a national hero, held up by the government as an example for the nation. A couple of weeks of competition in Canada had turned her from a nobody into a national hero.

Following the aftermath of the 1976 Olympics, Comăneci increasingly grew apart from the Károlyis – their controlling nature clashing with Comăneci's teen desires for freedom. She trained on and off, only putting in a hard stint just before the 1980 Olympics. She was rewarded with two more golds and two silvers. But, after that, she knew her career was over. Comăneci would eventually escape to exile in the United States, her eyes having been opened to a different way of life on tour as an athlete.

She attributes her success simply to the amount of hard work that she did as a child: 'People asked what was the secret of Romanian gymnastics – we just worked twice as hard as everyone else. Now everyone does it – which is why they are much better.'[7] She was put in an environment that encouraged a mindset of hard work, competition and an attitude of constant improvement. The structured mindset of her childhood is something that Comăneci still uses to this day; she still organises her day down to the last detail.

Everything in Béla Károlyi's Onesti programme was aimed at making her the best possible female gymnast, without consideration for her future health and well-being. It was reported by Rodica Dunca, who at age 15 represented Romania at the 1980 Moscow Games, that for girls who entered the programme, '"Hunger was our eternal enemy". Breakfast, she recalled, consisted of "one slice of salami, two nuts, and a glass of milk. In the evening we'd get the same menu, only without the nuts." The gymnasts' water intake was severely restricted, too, Dunca said, with desperate gymnasts driven to drinking toilet water'[8] as the programme sought to maintain their tiny physiques. During the Olympics in 1976, Nadia was 4 ft. 11 in. and weighed just 6 st. 2 lb., despite being 14 years old.

There is a growing number of allegations of cruelty and mistreatment in the Károlyi training system. In 2002, Dunca alleged that, while training with Károlyi, 'We were hit until blood was pouring out of our noses'.[9] Ecaterina Szabo, who won four golds and a silver at the 1984 Los Angeles Games, said once in an interview, '"I'll never forget the slaps in the face and the beatings I got from

Bela Karolyi."'[10]

Whether through desirable or undesirable means, the centralised training programme was a huge contributor in transforming Comăneci from an ordinary seven-year-old into one of the greatest gymnasts ever, just five years later. It was the external guiding force of a sporting body that created this transformation. It proved particularly important because of Nadia's background and the lack of access to high-quality coaching she would have had otherwise. By providing everything she needed for success, Nadia and her colleagues actually became some of the best-prepared young athletes to have a shot at success at world level.

It was not the creation of an environment where there were great facilities, education and expenses paid for that was the differentiating factor for Onesti – these were the prerequisites – this environment was combined with a truly radical coach who changed gymnastics as much as Nadia did. Béla Károlyi's focus on physicality moved women's gymnastics into the modern age and can be compared to how Richard Williams and Earl Woods developed athletes who changed their sport through their physicality. This combined with the sporting body brought success for young Nadia.

Even Károlyi and his Onesti girls could not dominate their sport in the same way that Jamaica has owned sprinting in the past decade; Jamaica has a population of just 2.9 million people,[11] but has won 11 of the last 12 sprinting gold medals (men and women's 100 m/200 m) available in the last 3 Olympic Games[12]; a domination now spanning 12 years that does not seem likely to end anytime soon. It has sparked heated debate about whether it is genetics, hard work or lifestyle that has led to such unparalleled success in high-profile events for a small nation.

What is clear is that the system that identifies, refines and maximises the talent of the next generation of sprinters plays a vital role. Jamaicans are obsessed with sprinting in the same way that Brazil is obsessed with football or India with cricket. The focus on sprinting has helped Jamaica continue to be the David that defeats the Goliaths on the world stage.

The headline act of this period of dominance is Usain Bolt. Bolt was a lanky eight-year-old kid living who had too much energy for his own good – despite the jobs given to him by his parents, as recalled in the Parents chapter. He was always found outside, playing endless games of cricket and up to all kinds of mischief on the dusty dirt roads of his home town. He was attending Waldensia Primary School, and spending most of his time doing what he loved most; pounding down the cricket wicket as a fast bowler, dreaming of being a star for the West Indies.

One day his PE teacher, Mr Nugent, brought him to one side.[13] He asked if he fancied taking on the 100 m at the upcoming sports day. 'Maybe' was Usain's reply. Him and his friends often ran against each other outside of school, but he knew he wasn't the fastest; that accolade went to Riccardo Geddes. That really made him mad, and he didn't want to be beaten in front all of his classmates.

But Mr Nugent saw real potential in Bolt and persisted in trying to convince him. 'You could be a sprinter', he said. Bolt remained non-committal. Mr Nugent tried bribing little Usain with food; he promised a box lunch if he beat Riccardo in the race. Bolt loved a box lunch - suddenly he was in, and deadly serious about winning. 'Suddenly there was an incentive, a prize. The thought of a reward got me all excited, as did the thrill of stepping up in a big championship.'[14]

As he crouched at the start line on the grass track, Bolt had never felt like this. This race was different to those with his friends because of the anticipation of the crowd about the race, and the bragging rights on offer. For the first time in his life, the outcome had significance and meaning to Bolt.

It was first to the shack at the end wins, with everyone watching on either side of the grass lanes. The starting call went. Bolt sprinted as hard as he could and managed to cross the line first. The sense of winning was a massive rush to him. He was hooked, and after that first positive experience, he began competing in track and field.

After winning more races in the parish of Trelawny, it was time for Bolt to leave primary school and attend high school. William Knibb High School offered him a sport scholarship due to his running ability. In return for the potential of having a running superstar in its ranks, William Knibb agreed to pay some of Bolt's tuition. The school had a great reputation for developing sprinters, with former students making it to the Olympics.

By his own admission, Bolt got lazy at William Knibb, and did the bare minimum training required to get by, relying instead on his raw talent. He focused on the 200 m and 400 m and tried simply to get through the mammoth training sessions of coach, sergeant-major Mr Barnett. Mr Barnett would make them do gruelling endurance sessions and 700 sit-ups a day. Eventually, these training sessions became too much for Bolt, and he started skipping them. As a result, he began progressing slower than his competitors. One of his rivals in his age group, Keith Spence, started beating him. This fired his competitive edge, and once again Bolt began to start training and competing like a champion. After all, 'Champs' were coming.

In his own words, Bolt believes that 'Champs was – and is – the heartbeat of Jamaican track and field success'. More formally known as the Inter-Secondary Schools Boys and Girls Championships,[15] Champs are the focus of the nation for five days a year; it is televised live and makes front-page news. The 30,000 tickets for each day at the National Stadium in Kingston are snapped up fast. It is bankrolled by sports companies wanting to sign up young sprinting talent for sponsorship deals. All of the top Jamaican government-funded coaches are also there, looking to see who has the potential that they can develop into senior athletes.

At the age of 14, Usain took part for the first time in 'Champs'. Expectations were limited given his age. First, he competed over 200 m in the under-16 age group. He sent his school mates wild with a silver in 22.06 seconds. Later in the day, in the 400 m, Bolt became a national sprint sensation by beating the favourite, Jermaine Gonzales, to take first place.[16] The focus of the attention and media acclaim was on Bolt. He loved it.

Even then, his coaches couldn't have predicted his meteoric rise. He would go on to become the youngest-ever World Junior Champion, where the age limit is under 18, just a year later. In his home nation of Jamaica, and aged just 15 years and 332 days, he took the gold in a time of 20.61 seconds. Now, the 15-year-old boy wonder was making international headlines, as all eyes focused on this incredible sprinting talent.

As a result of his performances, several US colleges offered Usain a place with a full sports scholarship, but he decided to stay closer to home and train in Jamaica. In 2003, he enrolled in the Kingston High Performance Institute, an International Association of Athletics Federations (IAAF) and Jamaica Athletics Administrative Association (JAAA) training facility in the city with full-time coaches paid to develop promising athletes. This guided his transition to the seniors, and the rest is history.

From the age of eight, Bolt did not once have to seek out professional training independently. The minute it was determined he had talent as a sprinter, he was offered support through the school system throughout his entire childhood. This included financial support, advice on how to handle all the fame and attention and education support to ensure he made it through school.

First, the Jamaican sprinting system picked up early that he had the potential to be fast. PE teachers like Mr Nugent are crucial at a grass-roots level for spotting those with raw speed and getting them involved in track and field. Mr Nugent saw Bolt's talent for sprinting and steered him in this direction, despite Usain's love for cricket (a reflection of Jamaica's obsession with track and field and something that perhaps helps explain the recent demise of the West Indies cricket team). This meant Bolt started sprinting and competing early and it put him on the conveyor belt that has been so effective at churning out international-standard athletes.

Having being talent-spotted at a primary-school level, Usain was then offered a high-school scholarship in return for him competing in track for the school. Wait, a sports scholarship from a high school? This indicates the value that the school system put on athletics, and the money they were willing to invest to develop the best talent from a very young age.

This kind of funding followed Usain throughout his career, primarily from benefits in kind. William Knibb not only covered his tuition to bring him to the school, but also offered him a top-class coaching team to develop his abilities. This was crucial in cajoling a 'lazy' Bolt to do enough training to continue his development.

The schools were also highly competitive with each other. When he was beaten in a track meet, Bolt didn't forget the loss easily. It ignited the desire to start training hard, improve his technique and get back on top. This intense competition at a school level undoubtedly pushed on the competitive types like Usain Bolt to improve themselves against their peers.

Never did this effect have more of an impact than in the crucible of 'Champs'. Not only did these high-school students have the ultimate competition to prove their worth against their competitors, but there were many other incentives to do well; they would be live on TV, the front page of newspapers, receive the adulation of the school, probable offers from US colleges and Jamaican running clubs, sponsorship from sports companies and selection for the Jamaican national junior teams. Is it any surprise that these athletes would go on to produce exceptional performances in these championships?

'Champs' also played a crucial role in bridging the gap between high school and senior competition for many Jamaican athletes, including Bolt. Often, athletes struggle to manage this transition as they are now without the structure of high school that has defined their lives for so long. Usain's transition was made easy by the offers he had from US colleges and the JAAA. He did not need to seek out support or think about his career. The best opportunities were laid out for him, both at home and abroad.

This can help us to better understand how Jamaica has managed to create so many sprint champions. Although not the fully centralised training systems of more extreme sporting bodies, the defined route for a child with potential through schools to professional sprinter, and the intense competition of the process, makes it much more likely that talent like Usain Bolt will be identified and cultivated to its maximum potential.

Usain can be lazy. He hates training and doesn't greatly enjoy the process of improvement like Nadia Comăneci. But he understands it is necessary for success, and what he really lives for is the sensation of winning and running fast. The Jamaican system ensured that this laziness did not ruin a once in a generation precocious talent.

So, what was the most important moment in Usain Bolt's childhood for his success? The moment that Mr Nugent bribed him with a box lunch if he raced in a primary-school sports day. The hardest thing for these programmes is getting the right talent into them; once in the system, it still requires a huge amount of work on behalf of the athlete, but the path to the top is much clearer.

The Romanian Onesti gymnastics team and Jamaica Athletics Administrative Association are two examples of sporting bodies that helped to produce athletes by providing everything they needed to create the environment for success from early childhood. Of course, Nadia Comăneci's upbringing was much stricter than Usain Bolt's, and the amount of control the sporting bodies exerted in their lives differs greatly. But both captured the essence of creating the right environment for success for children through high-quality coaching, financial help and creating competition amongst peers. It was the mentality of these two great athletes that differentiated themselves within this programme – Nadia's work ethic and Usain's competitiveness.

Countries are always looking to increase their medal hauls in major championships, and the activities of effective sporting bodies can help to achieve that. In recent years, the British Olympic Committee increased funding to great effect: overall funding for athletes competing in the Olympics increased from £58.9 m for Sydney 2000 to £274.5 m in Rio 2016.[17] By ensuring this funding is effective through creating competition between bodies for funding and tying funding to results, Team GB reached a peak performance at Rio 2016 with 27 golds, finishing an improbable second in the overall medal table, ahead of China. In essence, it's the same story as Jamaican sprinting, but on a larger scale – funding facilitates the creation of the right environments, and this is key to driving success.

Jamaica and Romania used sporting bodies to drive success at junior levels in sprinting and gymnastics respectively. By providing the support the athletes needed to flourish and ensuring that talent was identified and progressed along the conveyor belt towards the highest level of sport, athletes achieved greater success than they could have through trying to succeed on their own. But if effective sporting bodies are not in place, can child athletes develop a similar network of individuals to provide the same coaching, financial and facilities support? We will explore this in the next chapter.

8

Networks

Rather than being an individual, a child athlete is more of a 'solar system' of actors all contributing to the eventual success of the athlete. We began this book by studying the child athlete, the 'sun' at the centre: understanding the carefully cultivated Champion Mindset that is developed en route to becoming a champion athlete, the factor that lies at the very core of their success. We then looked at the nearby 'planets': the coaches, parents, school and siblings that directly shape the child's journey. Sporting Bodies was the first example of a peripheral planet, supporting from further afield – sometimes having a large effect, sometimes having none at all. Networks are another example of a peripheral orbiting planet: a supporting cast of actors that play a diverse range of roles from giving lifts to sharing some food under the counter at lunchtime. This network of individuals, who all help in their own way, can also be crucial to the development of athletes.

Accumulating thousands of hours of practice is no simple task. Even the most dedicated coach or parent will need a helping hand at some point to share the burden of supporting this alongside other adult commitments. This is where the networks that surround potential champions can become vitally important. We have considered the athlete's environment a number of times so far, looking at the main actors involved, but this also includes everyone the athletes interact with - from the bus driver to the school teacher. Some are inconsequential, but some are vital. This chapter is dedicated to better understanding them, and the roles that they can play.

Who you know can matter a lot in life: sport is no different. In certain sports, where there are few spaces available in the top tier of the sport and opportunities to reach them are sparse, this can be even more pertinent. Particularly in sports that carry a high cost, such as motor sports, who you know can be the difference between making it or not. Anthony Hamilton, Lewis' father, was acutely aware of this in his quest to break into the most elite of sports: Formula 1.

On a Sunday in December 1995, a 10-year-old Lewis Hamilton nervously approached the entrance to the annual Autosports Awards dinner in London with his father, dressed smartly in a green velvet jacket and patent leather black shoes.[1] He was invited after winning the British Karting Championship that year. Lewis carried his autograph book, with spaces for people to write their names, addresses and phone numbers. His father knew that they were about to meet the most important people in motorsport, and he wasn't about to miss the opportunity to ensure Lewis got their contact details. Motor sport can be difficult to break into – particularly for a family from Stevenage with no background in the sport. This was an opportunity to rub shoulders with the best.

Throughout the meal, Anthony would point out famous and important people to his son and send Lewis over to get their autograph. One of these was Ron Dennis, the head of McLaren. Lewis remembers their first conversation to this day:

> I walked up to Ron. I remember standing in front of him. I remember being so nervous and confident at the same time; nervous of speaking, but I also had my own self-belief, too. I knew what I wanted but I was not confident that I could speak the words properly. I was uncomfortable to the point that I really didn't want to say much. So I went up to him and said, 'Hello, I'm Lewis Hamilton. One day I'd like to be a racing driver and I'd like to race for McLaren'.
>
> Ron spoke to me for what seemed like ages, ten minutes or so, although I'm sure it was really just a minute or two. I remember looking in his eyes – and I never lost eye contact with him. He said, 'You have got to work hard at school. You have got to keep that spirit and keep going.' So I got him to sign my autograph book and I said, 'Can you also put down your number and address please?' and he said 'Okay'. He wrote down his address and said, 'I tell you what – phone me in nine years and I will sort you out a deal.' I said, 'Okay' and he wrote down his phone number. He just wrote 'Call me in nine years'.[2]

Ron Dennis would have an incredible influence over the career of Lewis Hamilton. He signed him in 1998 to the McLaren Mercedes Young Driver Support Programme which provided financial support to help pave the way towards Formula 1 for talented drivers:

> He was already successful in karting, so I knew he had talent, but it was more than that; I saw something in his eyes. It's like meeting a partner in life; you meet someone and you know that they're right; something about the body language, the eye contact, their presence, speaks to you. You just know. I just knew with Lewis.[3]

It had been a long road for Lewis to even be in the same room as Ron Dennis at the Annual Motorsport Awards gala dinner – and for his father, Anthony. In their first few years in motorsport, Anthony Hamilton had to work three jobs to fund his son's karting and still make ends meet. He worked for British Rail as a computer manager. When he came home from the day job, he would go straight back out the door and erect 'For Sale' signs for a local estate agent. He would also go door to door booking appointments for a friend's double-glazing company.[4]

McLaren's funding as part of the Young Driver Support Programme came at a crucial time when the Hamilton family were being stretched financially to their absolute limits. Motorsport is extremely expensive, and to give Lewis the best chance to succeed they had been travelling the country to compete in races, as well as maintaining the best possible kart they could. McLaren provided a much-needed financial safety blanket that allowed them to focus on the racing which Lewis and his father so dearly loved.

Beyond monetary gains, the programme helped build

important connections with one of the best known F1 teams. This contract included an option for McLaren to have Lewis as a Formula 1 driver, which they duly took in 2007. It was 12 years after Lewis' initial conversation with Ron Dennis – a little bit longer than the nine years he had promised. Ron remembers: 'We backed him. McLaren gave him the opportunity, but it was Lewis who took the opportunity; he worked hard and made sacrifices.'[5]

A year later, Lewis repaid McLaren's faith in him by winning the championship at his first attempt in one of the most iconic finishes in F1 history. In sixth position at the Brazilian Grand Prix on the final lap, needing fifth or higher to get the title, he overtook Timo Glock with just seconds of the race remaining to snatch the championship from home favourite, Felipe Massa, whose team was already celebrating. Lewis has remained one of F1's top drivers throughout his career and has added two further F1 Championships since.

It would have been easy for Lewis to attend the annual Autosports Awards dinner, have a nice time and leave with some good memories. But his father, Anthony, ensured that they maximised the potential to make contacts with the glittering guest list, and it paid dividends through building the connection that ultimately allowed Lewis Hamilton to succeed in his ambition to compete in Formula 1.

The importance of networks and knowing people who can help is something that is a repeated theme amongst these champions. In particular, for families who are not well-off but competing in sports with a high financial cost, supporting a child to compete can be a huge burden that networks can help to ease. Golf has many of the same problems as motor sport.

In Earl Woods' youth development manual *Training a Tiger*,[6] he reveals how important networking was in aiding Tiger's development. Although golf is stereotypically seen as an elitist sport, Earl has a different view, instead extolling the advantages of a sport where everyone from a 'plumber' to a 'CEO' plays the game side by side. Meeting these people is important, but Earl focuses on the need for 'maintaining them [contacts]. Encourage your child to exchange telephone numbers and addresses. The potential for networking while accompanying your child to tournaments is endless. Keep a record of the contacts you make. They will prove invaluable in the future'.[7] He highlights how many contacts would be happy to help Earl and Tiger stay at their homes when they travelled to tournaments around the country.

Earl Woods utilised his network far beyond free accommodation when travelling. He also used a variety of coaches to ensure that Tiger was exposed to different training methods and did not become too one-dimensional in his approach. Often, those who are taking unconventional routes through sport, far removed from the sporting-body path described in the last chapter, are forced to use networks to get the high-quality coaching and facilities they need for success – and actually result in future success by trialling new methods rather than copying the traditional ones.

Two other athletes forced to take an unconventional path were Alistair and Jonathan Brownlee. Triathlon was far from a mainstream sport when the Brownlee brothers became infatuated with it during their teenage years, and there certainly was no institutionally created path to success available. It is now one of the world's fastest-growing sports, helped by the success of the

Ironman brand and other extreme versions of the event. But in 2006, when Alistair Brownlee was 18 and Jonny Brownlee 16, the British Triathlon Federation had a membership of just 9,450.[8]

As a result, they had to create their own triathlon training regime. They sought coaches to help provide high-quality training across the three triathlon disciplines, as well as completing their own combined triathlon training. Luckily, growing up in the sports-mad heart of Yorkshire, they had plenty of options to pick from. Jonny puts this local network of coaches and opportunities at the centre of their success:

> For all that our parents gave us with their love of exercise and of the outdoors, our futures in sport were moulded by a colourful cast of characters that existed around the Leeds area as we grew up. Some were eccentric, others obsessive, and each of them, in their own way, was integral to the formation of the people and the athletes we have become.[9]

All kinds of opportunities fell their way. In 2000, 11-year-old Alistair was convinced by his mate at school, Nick Howard, to go and do a Bunny run. The Bunny run was a three-mile race across the fells in the Yorkshire Dales organised by Dave Woodhead, perhaps the most eccentric of characters in the Brownlee's childhood. He was the manager of the England Fell Running team, and his passion for the sport was overwhelming.

Alistair remembers it wasn't the glamour end of the sport:

> You began at an exposed gravel car park on top of a bleak moor, surrounded by small

disused quarries. Dave always claimed the pavilion where you registered for races was the highest cricket club in England, in which case I hope the players all brought two jumpers and were allowed to wear woolly hats. The course took you twisting in and out of the quarries, always heading up and down, never flat, but often very fast when gravity was on your side.[10]

Both brothers quickly improved in these races, taking part in individual and doubles events, and winning multiple junior Yorkshire titles. It developed the toughness that would eventually shine through in their triathlon races. But Dave never let them take themselves too seriously; he loved to add some fun to proceedings and embarrass the boys in any manner of ways when they won. The best prize Alistair has taken home? A balloon making kit.

Dave particularly loves to recount Jonny and Alistair competing in a two-person relay race where the baton was an actual egg – don't come back with it and you are disqualified. Jonny took the first leg, and 'as we came to the all-important handover the egg somehow slipped between his fingers and smashed on the turf. I had no choice – I reached down, scooped up the mess of shell, yolk and white and set off, eggshell spraying everywhere.'[11]

Fell running is notorious for being one of the hardest disciplines in running, only taken on by the hardiest. The toughness of the Brownlees' running ability was forged on the Yorkshire Dales in these races. The wild runs would help develop the X factor they would bring to triathlon events on the final leg.

Swimming lessons, despite Jonny's wishes, had always been part of their lives growing up. After training at a local leisure centre, both the boys were picked to be part of the City of Leeds club with its Olympic-sized pool. Their standard improved quickly as they competed alongside talented specialist swimmers. But the club was all-or-nothing about its eight training sessions a week, two hours at a time. Given the triathlon training they were doing, this was simply too much, and instead they moved to the City of Bradford under the tutelage of Corinne Tantrum, or 'Coz' as she is known. She was more flexible, fitting in around the boys' other training with a plan comprising six sessions a week.

Where the brothers got the most enjoyment from was their cycling training. It all started in a triathlon shop in Horsforth, just down the road from their house. It was run by a man called Adam Nevins. Adam passed on many words of wisdom and took the pair under his wing. He introduced them to the cycling group he was part of at the weekends, and the boys would regularly join them on rides. It never felt like training. Mostly, the boys simply saw it as heading off into the moors and having adventures.

Against the prevailing advice of the time, they would head off for '95 miles, 100 miles' round trips across the Dales at the age of 12. They'd be cycling in adult groups for hours, eventually getting to a café for a refuel of toasted teacakes before heading for home. The rides were riddled with attacks from the front, everyone loving the competition. They'd head off with mates across the Dales too, on long adventurous days where they would get hopelessly lost and cycle way further than they had planned. Cycling was always their fun element. 'Overtraining' was not a word they understood.

In all three disciplines, the Brownlees did not actively seek out the best elite coaches in the world; they developed alongside the people they knew locally – their network – and these people were vital to their success. They were lucky to grow up in Yorkshire, a unique place with a rich sporting history which had the facilities and coaches they needed for success. It was the combination of Dave, Coz and Adam that helped them reach an elite level while still in their teenage years. Whereas for Usain Bolt and Nadia Comăneci a sporting body was vital to create the environment for success, for the Brownlee brothers, it was their network that was crucial to creating this.

Like in Yorkshire for Triathlon, a certain culture around a sport in a particular location leads to many more champions than normal probability would suggest. You only have to look at the production of world-class footballers from Rio de Janeiro's favelas or China's production of world-class table tennis players to see this effect in action. This is different to the sporting bodies discussed in the previous chapter; there is no central controlling body. Instead, a sport is embraced by an entire population to such an extent that it becomes an integral part of the culture. The network of coaches, friends and family in such places can influence the development of world-class athletes.

Networks can play a vital role in helping children get the best coaching, playing partners and opportunities to train and compete. Whether this is by offering a different perspective on coaching or reducing the time or financial constraints that parents face, they all add up to aiding the athlete's progression. The good news is that the champions in this chapter did not come from highly networked families, as we traditionally think of those in the upper classes of society; instead, they worked hard to create a network of their own that provided the best opportunities possible to improve in their sport. As shown in the case of Lewis Hamilton, Tiger Woods and the Brownlees, they can prove pivotal in the journey to success for child athletes.

9

Practice

I assume most of the people reading this book currently play, or previously played, sport. I urge you to go out and practise your chosen sport for an hour. But don't do so aimlessly; practise under 1-to-1 coaching supervision and push repeatedly at the limits of your abilities. Focus on a specific area of your performance and try to improve it for an hour. Not 20 minutes or 40 minutes – a full 60 minutes.

I can guarantee that you will have two reactions following this. One, you will realise how much you can improve in just one hour of dedicated training to a specific skill. Second, you will realise how incredibly exhausting practising like this is.

There are many stories about how many practice hours top performing athletes accumulate. But truly understanding how difficult getting to the top is requires understanding the draining nature of practising in a way to maximise improvement. It is the consistent pushing of physical, mental and emotional limits that sets the top athletes apart. The Champion Mindset required for this is always forged in childhood.

It's why it's so difficult to pick up sports from scratch in adulthood and reach high levels of success unless you have developed this mindset in another endeavour. The Champion Mindset can be applied across sports – the ability to focus, respond to failure, maintain motivation and be intensely competitive is vital to practice and competition in any field. With the Champion Mindset in place, the sport-specific skills become the main learning curve.

Practice in sport has been widely studied and its role in success heavily debated. The most famous practice theory is the '10,000 hours rule' first coined by Malcolm Gladwell.[1] The theory suggests that 10,000 hours of deliberate practice is the amount required to become a world-class expert in any given field. There are no shortcuts, no ways around putting in this work. The evidence is from a study by practice expert Anders Ericsson about violinists which found that success was perfectly correlated to hours of practice. Those who went on to be virtuoso soloists had put in thousands more hours of deliberate practice than those who went on to become music teachers – with no exceptions (e.g. soloists who put in the same number of hours as the future music teachers, or future music teachers who had trained as much as the soloists).

This is only one chapter in a comprehensive book that has a different message at its core: that environment is crucial for the success of individuals. Gladwell's central point is that success is a result of the opportunities we have, our ability to work hard and the pervasive influence of the cultural legacy that surrounds us. In particular, he focuses on how opportunities often are arbitrarily determined by factors such as birthplace, and how important culture is, even though we do not interact with it. It is this combination that drives success.

But something about the 10,000 hours rule captured the imagination of those in sport, drawing both support and criticism. The likes of Matthew Syed's *Bounce*[2] and David Epstein's *The Sports Gene*[3] have powerfully argued for and against this rule respectively. To demonstrate the power of practice, Syed describes how in an academic study, a supposed innate ability such as being able to remember a string of numbers was increased through raw practice from a baseline of 7 until an individual could recall 82 digits. He goes on to apply this to the stories of 'Miraculous Children', those who seem talented at an extremely young age such as Tiger Woods and David Beckham. He concludes that they completed their 10,000 hours of practice by their mid-teens, and therefore were actually simply more advanced in their development through practice rather than having genetic talent that meant they were exceptional at a young age.[4]

Epstein argues instead that talent and genetics play a more significant role in sporting success than the practice doctrine acknowledges. He highlights the stories of two high jumpers at the 2007 Osaka World Athletics Championships: one, Stefan Holm, a dedicated athlete who put in his practice hours from a very early age to perfect his craft as a jumper. The other, Donald Thomas cleared seven feet at his first-ever attempt high jumping while in basketball shoes at university (he had accepted the challenge following an argument about his slam-dunking prowess). Thomas won the world championship gold, demonstrating that perhaps genetics sometimes is more important than practice. Epstein's point is not that practice is unimportant, but that genetics (both in terms of physical and mental characteristics) are important in explaining the difference in performance.[5]

In fact, the 10,000 hours rule is not really a rule that any of the above believe in its totality, but there are different views on the relative importance of practice vs genetics. Dr Anders Ericsson, the author of the original study Gladwell referred to, has devoted his life to studying how people improve and become experts in their chosen field.

Ericsson has responded to the 10,000 hours theory by stating that it is not a magic number, and that having this as a target misses the point. In fact, in his definitive book about practice titled *Peak*,[6] Ericsson said that it takes 10 years of practice just to become really good at something, and that athletes do not achieve their best performances until they have accumulated 20 years of high-quality practice. But he stresses it is the quality of the practice, rather than the sheer quantity, that is the real differentiator. This has been significantly underplayed in Gladwell and others' interpretation who have focused instead on a magic number.

According to Ericsson, the concept of 'deliberate practice' is the most efficient way to improve at anything – the gold standard of practice. Across all of his studies, it is the consistent techniques that experts have employed to reach the top of their field.

In *Peak*, Ericsson puts the coach at the heart of successful improvement through practice. He describes how in order to conduct Deliberate Practice, there must be the supervision of a coach, who uses "effective training techniques" to move towards "well-defined, specific goals" to improve the athlete's performance.[7] They subsequently provide constructive feedback in order to modify performance towards the defined goals.

For the student, the key is repeatedly pushing beyond current abilities, through uncomfortable practice that is not enjoyable. This can only be done by providing "full attention and conscious actions"[8] on the task in hand, responding to the feedback and seeking improvement. Over time, this develops the "mental representations"[9] that underpin sporting success.

This step-by-step improvement, repeatedly achieving goals that focus on where an athlete needs to improve, leads towards eventual success.[10]

Ericsson's Deliberate Practice is a type of practice few of us engage in and he believes that, often, this is a reason that 'normal' practice does not lead to improved performance; for example, it's why a club tennis player who trains once a week and plays a game at the weekend never seems to make any improvement after decades of following the same routine.

Ericsson's single view of deliberate practice as being central to all successes has been criticised for being too simplistic, and for not adequately reflecting the fact that there is a wide variety of environmental and hereditary factors that play an important role in determining success.[11]

It does, however, provide us with a cornerstone of principles to work with: that practice by experts has a focus on improvement driven by goals. It is engaged in by a totally focused student partnered with a coach knowledgeable in creating small improvements that together move the athlete towards a larger goal. This helps to create a mental 'representation' of the sport that means athletes trained this way can react and perform in a superior fashion to those without the same picture.

Did our champions practice in a similar way to

Ericsson's deliberate practice methodology, or was there anything different about their practice compared to the generally accepted view of the best way to improve?

Let's return to the cricket phenomenon from Mumbai, Sachin Tendulkar. We've already looked at how school helped to forge his skills but let us delve a little deeper into the day-to-day practice that turned him into one of the greatest batsmen of all time.

Tendulkar began to play cricket seriously aged 11 when he was part of coach Ramakant Achrekar's summer training camp. The young Sachin would take a 40-minute bus journey to Shivaji Park each day to take part. There were two sessions: one in the morning for three hours, and another similar session from afternoon to late evening. He describes the schedule as 'rigorous' and that he 'would be exhausted by the end of the day'.[12]

Following the summer training camp, Sachin moved to the Shardashram Vidyamandir school, where Ramakant was a coach. The quality of Sachin's training stepped up a notch. Competitive matches were played regularly, both internally at the school and in competitions with other schools. From the beginning, to challenge him, Sachin played in age brackets several years ahead of himself. With his talent obvious, coach Achrekar gave him special attention, always allowing him to bat at his favoured number four position in the batting order.

In his first summer holiday since joining Shardashram Vidyamandir, with no school work to do, the intensity of Tendulkar's cricket training increased to an astonishing quantity; out of 60 days in the summer, Sachin played 55 competitive matches, on top of all the other scheduled training sessions. Summer training days started at 7.30

a.m. with two hours of batting, split into five net sessions. After this, a match would begin immediately, running until 4.30 p.m. A 30-minute break would be held (where coach Ramakant would give Sachin some money for food and drink) and then, at 5 p.m., the evening session would begin, with another five net sessions.

In the final 15 minutes of the day, a rupee coin would be placed on top of the stumps. Every bowler would bowl at Tendulkar, with 60–70 fielders ready to catch him out. If he survived, he would be given the rupee. Sachin believes his intense concentration and skill to play the ball along the ground whenever possible were forged on this drill.

As a final act, his coach would make Sachin run twice around the large Shivaji Park, complete with pads and gloves. He would be left physically and mentally exhausted. But, crucially, he would be ready to take on the same again the very next day. Eventually, this mental and physical stamina would transfer to Tendulkar's ability to survive sustained attacks from the world's best international test bowlers and manage long innings out in the middle.

This high quantity and quality of training revolutionised Tendulkar's game. Under the one-to-one tutelage of coach Ramakant Achrekar, his game changed beyond recognition and he improved at an exceptional rate; his performances for the school reflected this.

Two cricket tournaments dominated the cricketing calendar for high schools in Mumbai: the Giles and Harris shields. The Giles Shield was for students aged under 14, while the Harris Shield was for players aged under 16. Both were known as proving grounds for the next generation of Indian cricket talent. Tendulkar played in both competitions during the 1987–88 season and did not fail to make an impression. During five games in the more senior Harris Shield, Sachin scored a staggering 1,025 runs, only getting out once. In the quarter-final, semi-final and final he scored 207 not out, 326 not out and 346 not out respectively. These astonishing performances, the likes of which had never been seen in the shield competitions, catapulted Tendulkar into the limelight and paved the way for him to make his senior first-class debut a year later, aged just 15. His meteoric rise did not stop there; he made his international debut a year later, aged 16.

Given how quickly he improved, how well does Tendulkar's practice routine fit Ericsson's deliberate practice philosophy? Firstly, he was practising outside his comfort zone every day. Ramakant constantly pushed Tendulkar, particularly towards the end of a tough practice day. The drill of Tendulkar batting while every bowler took turns to bowl at him, with 60–70 in the field to catch him out, is testament to Achrekar's desire to push Tendulkar out of his comfort zone, even if it meant many other players supporting him in doing so. Physically, he was tested by those final laps of Shivaji Park. This deliberate practice was critical to his quick development as a batsman.

Sachin's training was also under the supervision of a highly talented coach. As already alluded to, Ramakant Achrekar was highly regarded, but he also had results to back up his reputation. He developed a number of youngsters who went on to play for India, such as Vinod Kambli and Pravin Amre.[13] In 2010, for his services to sport, the president awarded him Padma Shri, one of the highest civilian awards in India.[14] He was also awarded the Lifetime Achievement award by then India coach,

Gary Kirsten. He is considered one of the best cricket coaches ever to grace India, if not the world. He focused these talents on Tendulkar to great effect.

Ramakant only identifies one trait crucial to good coaching:

> I guess the only definition of 'ideal' coach is one who is committed, fully and completely, to his students, and is one hundred per cent dedicated.
>
> I take a thorough trial of each student who comes to me, and observe his technique and style of playing stokes. I believe that every player should stick to his natural game, not change it, but try to improve it through constant practice and playing more games. My job as coach is to point out mistakes, to guide students into how best to correct their flaws while retaining their natural game.[15]

Ramakant saw providing feedback and facilitating practice as two of his most important roles in developing young players.

At its peak, Tendulkar was practising under the Deliberate Practice methodology with intensive repetition for over 11 hours per day. Over the two months of that first summer holiday at his new school, Tendulkar managed to practise for approximately 660 hours. Even during the early days during the summer camp, Tendulkar was training for 6–7 hours a day. It is easy to see how, over the course of five years, Sachin would go on to complete thousands of hours of practice. The coaching regime was also intense in nature, completed in a very short time frame, preventing any knowledge loss between sessions that can exist when athletes practise sporadically. The special thing about Tendulkar was his mental resilience in coping with this gruelling training regime; it took significant reserves of mental energy to be able to return each day for over 12 hours of intense deliberate practice-style training, resilience that would shine through in his professional career. The sheer amount of practice he fitted in between the age of 11, when he 'seriously started playing cricket' in his own words, and 16, when he made his international debut, was astonishing.

An interesting element of Achrekar's practice schedule was the variety of his training. Strictly from the deliberate practice philosophy's perspective, we would have expected Tendulkar to be given the most opportunities possible to play the greatest number of shots in an environment where feedback and technique modification could be made easily, i.e. practice heavily dominated by work in the nets, which would have provided this quick practice and feedback loop. Instead, Achrekar had a wide variety of games and scenarios to test his students.

This is likely to have had two impacts on Tendulkar's practice. First, having a variety of drills made it easier for Tendulkar to practise for a longer period of time. This is a common coaching tactic to increase the quantity of training – there are limits as to how long athletes can concentrate on a single routine or task. But by adding variety, more high-quality hours can be produced per day, aiding progress.

Second, variety helps to ensure that skills are well rounded. In particular, Achrekar focused on playing matches as a key way to practise. In many ways, this is inefficient training – two are batting out of a team of 11 at any one time and being out early in an innings can mean practice of just a few minutes in a whole day. But these practice matches exposed Tendulkar to a wider variety of situations that he would have to bat under – for example, times when his team was under pressure and needed runs, when the pitch was particularly slow, when the bowlers were dominating or when the weather was overcast. This helped to better prepare him for the senior ranks.

Tendulkar's rise from child prodigy to national hero was fast and is reminiscent of the way that Michael Phelps burst onto the swimming scene in his mid-teens. Phelps began swimming aged seven when, like most of us, he took his first swimming lessons because his mum said he had to. He started swimming every week from that moment onwards. His first significant deposit of training into the practice bank began when he was nine, when he began swimming for four 75-minute sessions every week, developing his lung and heart capacity.

In his book *No Limits: The Will to Succeed*,[16] Phelps describes how he believes that those endurance sessions in his younger years built a basic aerobic capacity for Bob Bowman to work with:

> I have a very high endurance capacity. Some of this is because I started swimming at seven and had, by the time that Bowman arrived at NBAC, put in four years in the pool. That was truly important in developing heart and lung capacity. They think now that you can really do a lot with a young athlete, before he or she hits puberty, to build endurance later on; longer swimming sets when you are young, for example. That's exactly what I did.[17]

Two years later, the arrival of coach Bob Bowman to

the NBAC made his previous schedule seem like child's play. Phelps started to train hard under his supervision, putting in two-and-a-half hour sessions every day of the week. These sessions were led in a disciplined manner, with the programme placing an enormous premium on attitude. It was unrelenting in its need for its students to follow Bob's demands.

Bob would always be challenging Phelps to dig deep, telling him 'Let's empty the tank'. Michael would always respond, constantly rising to Bob's high expectations through his competitive nature. Bob was struggling to find challenging enough sessions to match Phelps' appetite for work, even at his young age. At the age of 12, he moved to morning and evening practices. Bowman also worked hard on Phelps' strokes to iron out a number of bad habits he had developed. It was not an easy task to fight against the combative and intensely competitive Michael.

Bob knew that Phelps had the physical attributes and aerobic capacity to be a great swimmer. When Phelps was just 12 years old, Bowman told Michael's mother that he could swim in the Olympics if he worked hard and dedicated himself to the sport. Given this opportunity, Phelps dropped all other interests to solely focus on his swimming. He continued to work with Bob, whose high standards drove Phelps on a blazing path through the junior and senior ranks.

Bob's philosophy as a coach can distilled into two sentences: 'Set your goals high. Work conscientiously, every day, to achieve them.'[18] He would take working harder every day to a whole new level with his recruits. Bowman deeply believes in the advice from motivational speaker Earl Nightingale: 'You need to make a habit of doing the things that unsuccessful people don't like to do.' [19] There was a question that would constantly be repeated by Bob as a challenge to Phelps: 'Are you willing to go farther, work harder, be more committed and dedicated than anyone else?'

The answer was nearly always a resounding yes. Phelps writes that, for five years, between 1998 and 2003 (when he was aged 13–18): '[...] we did not believe in days off. I had one because of a snowstorm, two more due to removal of wisdom teeth. Christmas? See you at the pool. Thanksgiving? Pool. Birthdays? Pool. Sponsorship obligations? Work them out around practice.'[20] In his teenage years, he was averaging about 100 miles per week with astonishing consistency.

In an interview, aged 18, Phelps said:

> We train 365 days a year, it gives you that extra day of training that no one else has. There are not many clubs that train seven days a week, so that gives you that extra session every week where you can pick something up. I'm getting 52 more practices than everybody else is. That can make that little or big difference in the end.[21]

It was the definition of doing what others were not prepared to do.

This incredible dedication to training led to Phelps making it into the US trials in 2000, aged just 15. He finished in the top two in the 200 m Butterfly, qualifying for the Olympic Games that summer. He headed to Sydney as the youngest US man to be in an Olympic team for 68 years.[22] He was disappointed with a fifth place finish in the final, just missing out on a medal.

Having risen to prominence so early, Phelps could have followed the path of many others and succumbed to a number of potential distractions – Nadia Comăneci spoke about her struggles with motivation after her perfect 10s at the Montreal Olympics, drawn to other aspects of life instead.[23] But not Phelps; his trajectory continued to amaze. Just a year later, he took gold at the 2001 Swimming World Championships in Fukuoka, Japan, breaking the world record he had set a few months before in the US trials. In his next Olympic Games in Athens, aided by the decision to compete in multiple strokes, he won a staggering six golds and two bronzes[24] – an incredible feat for any athlete, never mind someone still only 19 years of age.

During his career, Phelps went on to win a collection of medals that is greater than most nations. He would retire in 2016 with 23 Olympic golds. If Phelps was a nation, his haul would put him 40th in the all-time Olympics medal table (as of 2016), just behind Jamaica and ahead of Ethiopia.[25] He also holds the record for most golds in individual events, and most Olympic golds in one single Games (eight). He has won a total of 83 medals in major international long-course competition, and personally holds three world records.

Phelps' training regime shows that this was far from a talented youngster who rose effortlessly to the top due to his physical attributes. The sheer quantity of training hours that Phelps put in is astonishing; he was training from the age of 11, under coaching supervision, for a minimum of two and a half hours. From the age of 12, he was doing two sessions a day, in the morning and evening. From the age of 13, he was training with no days off.

As for consistency? There is no parallel to Phelps. He had just *three days off in five years* such was his and Bowman's total obsession with their Olympic dream. Of course, it was clear that Phelps had potential and was progressing fast, and this was why there was the willingness from those around him to invest time and energy to achieve his goals. But the mental fortitude to practise intensely every single day cannot be underestimated. It is something that was unparalleled even amongst the other champion athletes studied.

No one was going to be left pondering about the swimmer that Phelps could become. Bob and Michael would regularly sit down and calibrate new goals, not just at the limit of Phelps' ability, but also at the limits of what anyone had ever done, even while he was still a teenager; this was their 'Dream Big' mentality.[26] The speed at which they moved from one goal to the next separated them from others.

This dedication and consistency was matched with a high-quality coach who demanded excellence, ensuring that the intensity was maintained. One of Bowman's most important decisions was to allow Phelps to compete in many different strokes. Not only did this later allow for Phelps to accumulate medals, it also helped to introduce variety that made it easier for Michael to train for longer. Bowman would also throw in drills to try and mix up the monotony of lengths, similar to how Ramakant Achrekar would play games and throw in new activities to keep Tendulkar interested. Again, variety of practice was vital in facilitating longer practice sessions.

We've specifically looked at the stories of how Tendulkar and Phelps developed through practice, but their stories are indicative of how practice was conducted during the childhood of all of our champions. It highlights some more general conclusions about how children develop into champions through practice.

The most striking element of any account of a champion's development in their sport is the sheer amount of practice they undertook on their way to the top – and how far removed this is from the norm. The majority of children attend one or two practice sessions a week in their chosen sport, with a competitive match during the weekend. The evidence from our champions suggests that training on every day possible was required to accumulate the hours needed to reach the top of their chosen sport. These sessions varied based on the demands of the sport; even Michael Phelps could not complete the 12-hour training days of Sachin Tendulkar. But consistency over a prolonged period of time is the key driver to accumulating lots of hours, rather than bursts of intense practice. Having the ability to do this brings us back to the Champion Mindset and the fortitude to target a goal for many days, months or even years.

As described in this chapter, the fingerprints of deliberate practice can be found all over the stories of our champions. Ericsson's theory begins with the assumption that there are effective training techniques and a structured progression path already available in the field in which an individual wants to become expert.[27] It is hard to think of a better example of this than sport, where training techniques are well established and encoded in youth development. He goes on to describe that deliberate practice takes place out of an individual's comfort zone, involving targeted performance against well-chosen goals that are measurable, with feedback loops that ensure performance can be reviewed and improved. It is in these areas that our champions excel and differentiate themselves from the majority of practice that children undertake in sport.

How do they manage this? First, take practising

outside of comfort zones. A deep competitive edge, combined with coaches that know how to set challenges just outside current abilities, means that working outside of comfort zones is the norm rather than an exception. There are countless examples of our champions being pushed out of their comfort zone through tough challenges, despite being talented – using tennis balls that didn't bounce, heckling while playing a golf shot, a field of 60–70 fielders trying to catch you out. These challenges happened in training, allowing these athletes to excel in competition.

Second, targeted performance with well-chosen goals were central to the development of all the athletes. Interestingly, it depended on the athlete whether these were externally or internally motivated. Some athletes trained to constantly improve themselves, their technique and their performance, often bursting on to the competitive scene with skills far superior to their peers. Others were deeply motivated by championships, titles and events, and modified their performance to meet these goals. However, all were supremely driven to improve, the core competitiveness that is the bedrock of the Champion Mindset.

Third, feedback loops were central to our champions' development. This comes in two forms. Coaches and instructors played a vital role in providing constant feedback, delivering this in an encouraging rather than damaging way to the young athletes. The children themselves also quickly learned how to analyse their performance, understand their mistakes and adjust improve. During practice sessions, Tiger Woods will stand still after hitting a shot, mentally running through his performance and providing self-feedback. This is an internalised skill that these athletes develop.

In describing how closely our champions adhere to these deliberate practice requirements, we have discussed the role of coaches. There is a striking and perhaps surprising commonality amongst our champions: except in very rare cases, none of the athletes trained alone. Coaches were practically ever-present during their sessions. Full-time professional coaches were nearly always there and showed an incredible level of dedication to spend hours with their future protégés. For some, like Sachin Tendulkar, this developed into an all-encompassing relationship that was similar another parent.

Why is it that these individuals did not have significant time training on their own? Training at the limit of your abilities requires considerable mental and physical exertion. Training alone, and pushing yourself to your limits, is even more difficult. Combined with setting goals and providing feedback, coaches' roles were so critical that it is hard to replace them singlehandedly, particularly as a child. Deliberate practice is much easier with someone by your side.

One of the roles that coaches also played was ensuring that practice was varied enough to be enjoyable. Deliberate practice is tough, never mind the mental numbness of repeating the same task. By varying sessions, and making it fun, kids were willing to practise for a much longer period of time. This variety was key to engagement and kids pushing themselves for long periods of time. For example, Phelps learning many different strokes and having to complete new drills helped to improve the longevity of his sessions against the inherent monotony of swimming lengths.

Similarly, the presence of other skilled children to practise with and against is important. For competitiveness to be effective, those immediately around a child during practice must be of a good standard. Otherwise, becoming the best at a sport in the locality will not require great skill, and motivation to keep practising will fade. For Sachin Tendulkar, entering into a new school with many talented kids, some of whom would also go on to play professional cricket, this was definitely vital to improving his practice.

This non-individual account of how our champions made it is counter-intuitive to the folklore stories we like to tell. Often, there is a stereotype of a young child obsessively practising their sport on their own, kicking a football against the wall of a house, running endless laps of a running track or making basketball shots. In reality, the nucleus of the improvement lay in the long sessions with the coach and skilled peers, pushing at their limits for hours on end. It was in collaboration with others that the champions were truly forged.

We have discussed the quantity and quality of training needed for success. What we have not discussed is what athletes must forego – the significant sacrifices in other aspects of the child's life. Throw mandatory school into the mix, and suddenly there isn't much time in a child's life for anything else. Understanding this implication, and for a child to decide about how they want to spend their time at a very young age, is difficult to say the least. It is something that many struggle with, right up to their professional career. We will look in more detail about sacrifices later in this book.

Practice is the most important differentiator for what our champions did during their childhood that others did not. Their dedication is unparalleled, delivering consistent deliberate practice for years on end, under the direct supervision of talent coaches and competing against skilled peers. It is difficult, hard work, but absolutely mandatory for becoming a champion.

10

The History of Practice

In a 2014 TED Talk,[1] writer David Epstein asked his audience, 'Are athletes really getting faster, better and stronger?' Evidence shows that world records are falling at a higher rate than ever before. But stepping back, it seems unlikely that, at a species level, our genetics are improving at such a quick rate to cause this phenomenon. So, what is behind this trend?

Epstein highlights three key factors to explain this. The first is changing technology, a trend we have seen across all sports. The likes of better running tracks, more efficient bikes and better streamlined swimsuits are helping to shave seconds off records. Second, he highlights that genetic suitability also plays an important role. The world-class athletes of the modern era are more genetically specialised to their event, such as swimmers having larger wingspans and jockeys becoming smaller. Finally, Epstein highlighted the importance of our changing mindset towards the limits of human ability; increasingly, it seems like the boundaries of human potential are less constrictive than we thought. All three combine to lead to this continuing succession of falling records.

All of Epstein's factors are undoubtedly important, and empirical evidence supports his argument that improved technology, genetic suitability and changing mindset contribute to the continuous falling of world records. However, there is another factor that has not been given its due attention by Epstein: the volume of training has increased remarkably. The best athletes in the world today have completed many more hours of practice in their sports than the best athletes in the world of yesteryear. This change is even more substantial in the childhoods of our champions. This increased quantity is combined with a general higher quality of training as practice methods have become more sophisticated. This has been a huge contributor to the continuous falling of world records.

One of Epstein's examples during his talk was the ultimate believed constraint of human ability: being able to run a mile in under four minutes.

In the early 1940s, Swedes Arne Anderson and Gunder Hagg traded ownership of the mile world record, eventually getting it down to 4:01.4 in 1945 whilst racing was curtailed for many athletes due to World War II.[3] A glut of athletes over the course of the next decade managed to record similar times in the low 4:00s, but breaking the barrier remained elusive.

In the race to be the first one to break the four-minute barrier, Roger Bannister was Britain's best hope. He was in competition with Australian John Landy, who ran

164

4:02.00 in early 1954 and Bannister was sure he would break the record soon. The public was gripped by the race to see who, if anyone, would be the first to break the barrier. Bannister had a couple of failed attempts at the distance, before a fateful afternoon in Oxford.

On 6th May 1954, Bannister prepared himself to take on the challenge in a meet between the English Amateur Athletics Association and Oxford University on a blustery day at the university's Iffley Road Stadium. He had two pacemakers to help him on his latest attempt: friends Chris Brasher and Chris Chataway, who were looking to run three minutes for the first three laps to give Bannister the best chance to break the record. Bannister knew that he had the ability to break the record, but the question was whether he could achieve the result on the day.

The gun went off for the race. Bannister set off with his pacemakers immediately to the front. They quickly left the rest of the field in their wake; this was not a competition against anyone but the clock. Chris Brasher took the lead for the first two laps, taking them through 58 seconds for 400 m and 1:58 for the half mile – a little quick, but not far off. He peeled away, and Chris Chataway took the lead, blowing like a steam train as he tried to keep up the pace. Despite his best efforts, he began losing speed. They went through the bell for the final lap in 3:01. Bannister was going to need a huge effort to produce a sub-60-second final lap after such a slow penultimate 400 m.

Bannister was all alone on the final lap, exertion written all over his feverish movements.[4] The grimace on his face was etched deep as he willed more out of his body, lifted by the roars of the crowd as they urged him towards the finish. Into the final 50 m, his arms were flailing, legs still producing long, elegant strides. He ran through the line, face in anguish, to be caught by two men to keep him upright. The bulbs from the cameras flashed as the media hoped to capture a special moment.

Everyone waited with bated breath for the confirmed time. It was close. Norris McWhirter began to announce the results:

> "Ladies and gentlemen, here is the result of event nine, the one mile: first, number 41, R. G. Bannister, Amateur Athletic Association and formerly of Exeter and Merton Colleges, Oxford, with a time which is a new meeting and track record, and which—subject to ratification—will be a new English Native, British National, All-Comers, European, British Empire and world record. The time was three—"

The rest of the time was drowned out by the wild celebration of the crowd which had just witnessed history in the making. His time of 3:59.4 would be etched in history forever – the first sub 4-minute mile.

Donald McRae of *The Guardian* remembers what a momentous moment it was:

> Until then, there had been a widespread belief that it was physically impossible for a man to run the mile in less than four minutes. People claimed the human body would burst amid such a trial of speed and endurance. Bannister, slipping into his best Inspector Clouseau-style accent, remembers that, "a Frenchman once said to my wife, 'but 'ow did 'ee know 'ees heart would not burst?".[2]

Bannister became a famous figure in the pantheon of

athletics heroes primarily due to this one moment. Despite how momentous this event was at the time, good high-school athletes now dip under the four-minute barrier. The time would not see you even reach most national standards in the 1600 m, never mind the Olympic standard. The current men's world record of 3:43.13 held by Hicham El Guerrouj of Morocco (set in 1999)[5] and would surely be lower if the 1500 m was not the favoured distance at international level. How could such a monumental achievement become so commonplace in the space of 50 years?

To understand this, we need to understand a little bit more about how Bannister became the first sub 4-minute mile runner.

Bannister was not a sporting prodigy during his early childhood.[6] He took part in school sports with some success, but was not exceptional in terms of his performances. In the autumn of 1946, at the age of 17, he decided to join his university athletics club in Oxford. He had never before worn running spikes or run on a track. His training was light, only having three half-hour training sessions a week. Once he started to run regularly, it was noted by his coaches that he had promise.

In 1950, after a succession of defeats, Bannister's determination hardened and he started to train much more seriously. He was now under the tutelage of influential coach Franz Stampfl, who introduced a modern approach to training that focused on a mixture of interval and anaerobic training.

This training contrasted with the dominant theory of the time; the common view was to save oneself for the 'Corinthian Effort'. This gentleman theory did not believe in training, but instead in rest in preparation to push the body as hard as possible in competition – coming up with one effort to be able to defeat opponents by simply running harder than everyone else. It was only after the introduction of more sophisticated training methods that competitors realised that conditioning was an important element of preparing for a competition.

After two more years of hard training following his undergraduate degree from Oxford, Bannister was selected for the 1952 Olympics in Helsinki with high hopes for a gold medal. Instead, he suffered an extremely disappointing fourth place finish. He considered quitting to focus on his studies to become a doctor but instead decided to keep training with a new goal in mind – the elusive four-minute mile.[7] His decision was justified at the Oxford University track two years later.

Bannister's record took significant sacrifice in terms of time and effort alongside Stampfl's radical new training techniques. As he explains 'People still say, "Did you actually mean to do it?" It's as if they imagine I woke one morning and thought, "should I go punting on the river or run a four-minute mile?" They don't know I had run 20,000 miles in eight years of preparation.'[8]

After his competitive running days were over, Bannister went on to become a successful neurosurgeon in London, spending his life in the profession. However, after his death in 2018, Bannister has always been remembered for that special feat in 1954.

Fast-forward almost exactly 25 years from Bannister's record-breaking day, and another young British middle-distance runner by the name of Sebastian Coe stood on the line at the beginning of the famous 'Golden Mile' race in Oslo.[9] The meet was renowned for its history of breaking world records. After storming to the 800 m world record 10 days earlier, Coe was ready to take on the headline event: the mile. The British Press were there to document it, hopeful rather than expectant of another special moment by a Briton to rival that of Bannister.

The event had brought together the best milers from across the globe and promised to be a true showdown. Coe was far from a favourite but was the 'danger man, as no one knows how good he can be', as described by commentator John Walker. His personal best was the third slowest in the field and his endurance was likely to struggle in the later stages due to his preference for shorter distances. But Seb, along with his coach, thought he could win. He rarely ran the mile in competition, yet it seemed a great opportunity given his performances in the 800 m.

The race began with a rapid pace, and many of the 13-strong field were quickly separated from the leaders. Coe remained in the lead pack, feeling relaxed. Entering into the home straight of the penultimate lap, in his own words, Seb thought, 'Sod it, I'll go it alone.' He flew from the front of the pack with speed that could not be matched, running a magnificent final lap to not only win the race but break the world record with a time of 3:48.95. He became one of British Athletics' biggest sensations overnight. Twice more in his career he would go on to lower the world record over the mile.

Coe's world record was over 10 seconds quicker than Bannister's, despite being just 25 years later. How could he achieve such a fast time so soon after Bannister broke the impossible barrier?

To understand this, we need to also look back into

Coe's childhood. Coe's early running story is a world away from Bannister's. He professes a deep love for running, remembering fondly the feeling of freedom and speed when he ran. In his early days living in Alcester, Warwickshire, he remembers sprinting from field gate to field gate ahead of the car to let it through during their long walks through the rolling countryside – the original interval training.

Coe began running competitively following a move to Sheffield due to his father's work. Inspired by a visit to his new school from some British Olympians, he decided to join local running club Hallamshire Harriers with a friend. He threw himself into running for the club. Seb remembers, as with many Harriers clubs, cross country running was 'in its DNA'. He would run with the seniors across the Yorkshire Moors, and by the age of 14 rarely was left behind by the club's best.

Coe describes cross-country running as the making of him; running across the moors in those early days was harder than anything he has done since. His love for running meant he took every opportunity to participate that he could. Coe remembers:

> On Saturday mornings I'd run for the school and sometimes run for the club the same afternoon – two cross-country races in a day is unheard of now. I'd be home for *Match of the Day* and barely twelve hours later I'd be back down at the club for the Sunday run, and then there were the training sessions on Tuesdays and Thursdays...[10]

Seeing the potential that Seb had, his father, Peter, began to research athletics training. Although he had no prior knowledge of running, he taught himself using manuals and speaking to local coaches. His engineering background meant that Peter took a formidably analytical approach to the task.

Peter began to coach Seb and decided to not adopt the maximum mileage training methodology that was the dominant doctrine of the time. Instead, he focused on less mileage at a faster pace, eerily similar to how Stampfl had trained Bannister. This meant that the training was heavily focused on speed endurance and interval sessions.

Typically, Coe would run 40 x 200 m sprints with 30 seconds recovery, or 6 x 800 m intervals with short recovery times. Sheffield's hills added a further handicap to these sessions: the three-and-a-half-mile gentle climb of the Rivelin Valley Road became as familiar to young Seb 'as the garden path'. Always behind him, encouraging and cajoling, was his father in his Ford Cortina Estate car. 'As my coach, Peter's job was to get the best out of me, which he undoubtedly did, sometimes pushing me to the limit.'[11]

For the next 20 years, two hour-long sessions per day would become the default schedule for Coe, with his father as coach. This was in addition to the cross-country running and club training sessions he would complete. Later, in his teens, weightlifting would also become an important part of the regime.

His dad had a willing student in Seb, who followed this regime despite the unease of his club. Coe usually placed in the top three positions of cross-country races even before his father became involved. Now someone was challenging the way that he was being trained, despite his relative success.

But his father's approach paid dividends, with Coe

quickly climbing the national junior ranks before arriving on the world scene where he continued to achieve great success. His career would include obtaining four Olympic medals, winning gold in the 1500 m and silver in the 800 m at both the 1980 Moscow and 1984 Los Angeles Games. He would also set a total of 11 world records across middle-distance running events.[12]

In fact, he is now better known for his career in sport after being a runner. Coe would go on to head the successful London bid to host the 2012 Summer Olympics and became chairman of the London Organising Committee for the Olympic Games. Afterwards, he became chairman of the British Olympic Association between 2012 and 2016. In August 2015, he was elected president of the IAAF, where he still resides as the most influential individual in world athletics. He was also given a lordship in 2000.[13]

Just over 25 years apart, the quantum leap in childhood training between Coe and Bannister could not be more evident. Bannister took part in school sports and other outdoor activities that a child usually would, with no specific focus on training as a runner. He had never even run on a track before he joined the university athletics club at 17. Bannister describes how the majority believed in the Corinthian ideology, that a huge effort was the key to success. This was dispelled by his coach Herr Stampfl, who introduced interval training and a more dedicated programme of improvement. After a number of years under his tutelage and hard training, Bannister was able to break the four-minute barrier and was immortalised in athletics folklore.

In contrast, Coe was in serious training from his early teens. A high quantity of training was driven by running for his school, his athletics club and separate training sessions with his father. Similar to Bannister, his father's focus on interval training and speed work helped to elevate his performance further. In his teens, Coe was training for much longer, and harder, than Bannister – who at the same age had not even tried on a pair of spikes.

The quantity and quality of specialised training in Coe's early years contributed to a remarkable improvement in performance, with 10 seconds wiped off the world record for the mile, 25 years later. This was despite protestations in the 1940s that the four-minute mile represented an impossible barrier – in fact, it proved to be just the beginning of a succession of records falling.

It is hard to underestimate the way in which training has improved over the past century across a multitude of sports. With better knowledge-sharing options, most notably the internet, learning training techniques and how to apply them has never been easier.

The most extreme example of this is the astonishing story of Julius Yego.[14] Growing up in rural Kenya, Yego developed an interest in javelin throwing. With no access to coaches, like many looking to learn a new skill, he turned to YouTube.[15] Watching videos of the likes of Jan Železný and Andreas Thorkildsen taught him how to throw, along with tutorials of how to work out in the gym. He quickly ascended to become Kenyan national champion, eventually taking a gold in the 2015 World Championships and a silver in the 2016 Rio Olympics. He now has the nickname 'Mr YouTube'.

The 'standing on the shoulders of giants' phrase is often used in science. It refers to how scientists' research is always building on those before them. To reach the pinnacle, you must understand the field as known up to that point, before edging it further forward. This continual process increases the known field, making it harder to reach the top.

The same 'standing on the shoulders of giants' effect happens in sport. As world records fall and athletes extend performance beyond the known field, the requirements to reach the top increase. In turn, this continues to increase the demands on quality and quantity of practice in childhood. Now, children are having to start at a younger age than previous generations simply to fit in the amount of training required to reach the top level.

Inevitably, this will cause friction as the demands of other aspects of life also need to be considered. In the most extreme cases of Tiger Woods and the Williams sisters, these athletes were trained essentially from birth for their sports. Moral and ethical questions will persist as long as this is the case. The Netflix documentary *The Short Game*[16] followed six- and seven-year-old golfers competing in the 2012 US Kids Golf World Championship, showing the pressures and strains that training and competition holds for them. It is an eye-opening insight into the pressures for junior athletes at the top of the game.

The need for high volume and specialised training at an early age means the role of mentality in childhood will become increasingly important. Ensuring kids remaining engaged and enthused with sports is going to become more difficult for two reasons: First, as the amount of training required to get to the top becomes more extreme, engaging kids to take part when the barriers to success are high is going to be a battle. Second, the sheer volume of training required will need careful managing to ensure variety and fun, otherwise children are simply going to quit.

The example of Roger Bannister and Sebastian Coe breaking the mile world record 25 years apart, shows how differences in training during childhood contribute towards the trend identified by Epstein that world records are falling at an increasingly fast rate. As standards continue to improve, this will only continue, with children having to pack in more training at a younger age to make it to the top. Managing this will be crucial for the champions of tomorrow.

11
Luck

The contributing factors to the sporting development of the champions considered so far have all been controllable. The mindset can be crafted; it is not genetically given. The environment can be shaped through careful selection of the right individuals. Practice is the most controllable, and there are clear rules to follow in order to make the best progress. But it would be foolish to suggest that this is the whole picture of developing a sporting champion. We don't have any control over many aspects of our lives – and this is only amplified in the lives of young children. This section looks in more detail at those factors outside of our control that can completely derail the most competitive, dedicated and resilient child wanting desperately to be a sporting champion.

No matter how carefully you prepare and plan for an outcome, you will always be impacted to some extent by luck. We most commonly think of the negative outcomes that luck can bring, such as getting injured during a key competition. But luck and random events can also help in a positive way, where a chance encounter may offer the opportunities to move ahead of the pack.

The presence of randomness means that many of our champions consider how to improve the 'likelihood of success' rather than targeting success itself. All the factors that contribute towards success – a dedicated coach, the right facilities, a supportive school – simply increase or decrease the chance of success. There is no way of guaranteeing it. Being aware of this often removes much of the pressure too.

One individual who was on his own journey towards sporting success during his childhood was Benjamin Collett.[1] Ben was born in Bury, just outside Manchester. In line with the long tradition in the North West of England, he played football. In 2001, aged 17, he signed a contract to be a trainee with Manchester United, one of the biggest clubs in the world. The future looked bright for a player who was being compared to Manchester United legend Ryan Giggs.[2]

The season after signing his training contract, Ben became a regular in the under-17s, and quickly made the leap to the under-19s. In the 2002–03 season, he was awarded the Jimmy Murphy Young Player of the Year Award, a trophy that has been handed to the likes of Marcus Rashford, Giuseppe Rossi and Paul Scholes down the years.[3] The season also brought team honours, with Ben playing a vital part in helping Manchester United win the prestigious FA Youth Cup.

'Ben had been the outstanding player in the academy in terms of ability and creativity, his genuine understanding of the game, and outstanding work ethic and ability to learn', Manchester United coach Paul McGuinness said. He went on, '"Ben set an extremely good example to all his colleagues, and we wanted some of that to rub off," he said. "He was a model to other players: a reliable player who always gave 100 per cent every match."'[4]

A week after the FA Youth Cup Final, Ben played in a reserve team match against Middlesbrough. But, part way through the game, Ben suffered a horrific tackle from Middlesbrough midfielder Gary Smith. The tackle broke his leg in two places.

In that one tackle, Ben's career was effectively over. Despite intensive rehabilitation from Manchester United, he never reached the levels he had played at previously. He would go on to play short spells at unknown teams New Zealand Knights and AGOVV Apeldoorn, before being forced into retirement.

In May 2008, he began legal proceedings against Smith and Middlesbrough for the loss of earnings resulting from the tackle. Many of Manchester United's legends testified to his potential, and his likelihood of having a successful career at United.

Gary Neville, in the subsequent court hearing, spoke of Ben's potential:

> He was never outclassed, or in a position where he couldn't cope. But for the injury, I would have expected him to become a top-level football player. It was a certainty. Desire was something he had in abundance. He was the type of character that would have come back again, and again and again.[5]

'I thought the boy showed fantastic focus, a great attitude to work hard, and they are qualities to give any player an outstanding chance in the game,' Sir Alex Ferguson was quoted as saying about Ben at the hearing.

He even likened his qualities to Bryan Robson and Roy Keane, the two former United captains.[6]

Former England coach Howard Wilkinson was also called as an expert witness: 'In my opinion, his chances of making the Premiership were twice as great as his becoming a Championship player – and that's not a hunch.' [7]

The case was settled with Collett receiving an initial sum of £4.3 million in compensation,[8] despite never having played a first team game. That one tackle in a reserve-team game against Middlesbrough snatched his career away from him and prevented him from pursuing his dream of becoming a Manchester United legend. It was pure bad luck that prevented him from not realising his dream – a cruel reminder of how we can always be the victim of random bad luck.

Unfortunately, the chance of injury in football is actually the highest of any sport in the UK – 'Despite common misconceptions, football is revealed to be the UK's most dangerous sport with 1 in 5 admit to having suffered a serious injury whilst playing... Despite the popular belief that rugby is one of the most brutal UK sports, the study shows that people are four times more likely to suffer an injury playing football'[9], reports Benenden Healthcare. Bad luck can strike anyone on their journey to becoming a sporting champion.

Luck is something that we also need to consider in positive terms. While there are no examples of fairy-tale 'Scout Picks Wonderkid From Obscurity' stories in our rostrum of champions, luck definitely played its part in a subtler way.

Given the high volume of quality coaching required during childhood, it is incredibly beneficial to have a top coach helping early in a child's development. Some actively sought out great coaches from Day 1, most notably with the Williams and Woods parents becoming excellent coaches themselves. A number happened to fall into the hands of truly world-class coaches through local sport. This was the case for, arguably, the greatest coach–athlete partnership of all time: Bob Bowman and Michael Phelps.

As we saw in the Coaches chapter, Bob Bowman was the crucial figure in Phelps' becoming one of the youngest Olympians of all time, and eventually becoming the most decorated. Bowman methodically pushed Phelps to his absolute (superhuman) limits and managed to progress him to the elite level at just 14 years of age when he made his first Olympic Games. Bowman was knowledgeable, ambitious and the perfect personality fit for a young Michael Phelps with huge competitive drive and determination. But the partnership was far from a planned one.

Bob's story begins when he was growing up in South Carolina. A talented individual, he was someone for whom success appeared to come easily in a wide range of disciplines, from academia to sport. That was apart from one aspect of his life: swimming. In some ways, this motivated him more to pursue this. He still managed to become an impressive swimmer, obtaining a swim scholarship to Florida State University and competing for the 'Seminoles'.[10] In his final year he was team captain, as well as competing in the Nationals in the 100 m fly. While at Florida State, he majored in development psychology.[11]

As a recent graduate, Bowman began coaching at a local swimming club, and quickly discovered it satisfied his appetite for achievement and success. He decided on a career as a swimming coach and threw himself into the sport. His impatient and demanding nature meant he struggled to find a club to match his ambitions. He was an exacting coach who would never accept less than 100 per cent. In nine years, this desire for progress led him to coach in seven different places across five states.

In 1995, Bowman finally had the opportunity to apply for his dream job when the position of head coach of Dynamo Swim Club in Atlanta became available. With his wide experience, he hoped desperately to get the job. But he was left disappointed, not being selected for the role.

Bowman gave up on trying to make it in the sport. He instead turned to a different passion; rather than training athletes, he would train thoroughbred horses. He figured he would get a degree from Auburn University to give him the skills he would need for success in this new challenge. As John Doe wrote in ESPN magazine, 'Bowman came to North Baltimore on his way to veterinary school. Bowman planned to quit coaching after a pair of Olympic hopefuls left him before the Atlanta Games, but North Baltimore's Murray Stephens offered him $30,000 to coach for one more season'.[12]

It was soon after that Bob met a young boy at the club by the name of Michael Phelps, already putting in a couple of hours in the pool per day and with a physique that suggested plenty of potential. He set to work developing him and his classmates, and the swimming bug bit again. Fast forward to the present day, and Bowman has now developed 3 individual national champions, 10 national finalists and 5 US National Team members from NBAC.

Prior to his transformation of NBAC, Bob was a respected coach in swimming circles, but he was not seen as one of the best. His rejection from his dream job in Atlanta showcases this. If an ambitious kid was wanting a swim coach to give them the best possible opportunities of becoming a national champion, Bob Bowman would not have been top of the list.

In fact, it was luck that played a big part in ensuring that the best coach for Phelps arrived at the right time. Michael's mother, Debbie, didn't pick out Bowman. She took him to a good club, which increased his chances of finding high-quality coaching significantly, but the fact that Bowman was there, a coach who fitted Michael's personality as a swimmer, was due to a number of random events.

The way Bowman arrived in Baltimore could not have been more fortuitous, with him getting rejected from Dynamo Swim Club and instead pursuing a different career path breeding horses. It was this series of events that led to Phelps getting the perfect coach; one who would train him hard and push to his very limits on a daily basis. Luck played its part in matching the two together. It shows how chance can play a vital role in defining the opportunities for improvement in children.

Why does luck perhaps play a more crucial role in childhood? There are two reasons for this: lack of control and path dependency.

First, the reality is that children have very little control over the majority of their lives. They are hugely influenced by their guardians' decisions. If their parents move to take a job in a different part of the country, moving away from the perfect coach, this is simply bad luck for the child – they cannot influence this at all. Their sphere of control is significantly smaller compared to when they are older and they can make more decisions for themselves.

The second reason why luck has a disproportionate impact on child success is path dependency. Random events, even if they seem small at the time, can have a big influence over the long run. This is the theory of path dependency. Path dependency states that what happened in the past influences the future – in short, that history matters.

What may seem like an obvious idea has a significant impact on the likelihood of sporting success in childhood, as explained eloquently by Malcolm Gladwell in *Outliers.* In the opening chapter, Gladwell explores why there is a strong correlation between the top Canadian ice-hockey players and their birth date being in the months of January, February and March.[13]

The reason why? The cut-off for junior age groups in Canadian Ice Hockey is January 1st. Right when these children started playing ice hockey, those who were born in January were likely to be slightly more physically developed than those born in September, given that even a few months at the age of five or six can have a huge impact on physical development. Therefore, these older kids were 'talent-spotted' to play for regional and national teams due to their perceived ability, which was actually due more to physical development. This led to further increased amounts of training by high-quality coaches in a competitive environment. The cumulative effect of this meant that children who were born in the first three months of the year accelerated away from their peers in terms of development, and by the time we see a sample from the Canadian senior ice-hockey teams, the majority are born in the first three months of the year.

This shows how seemingly inconsequential differences at an early age can change the trajectory of sporting success. Ill on the day of a trial for an academy at a young age? This misfortune could cost you a place at the academy, meaning less high-quality training for this season, making it harder to get in at the next trial – the gap growing ever wider as others develop faster.

A great example of this comes from the very start of Sachin Tendulkar's story.[14] Sachin had begun playing seriously and trialled for a prestigious summer camp in Mumbai. He was nervous, played poorly and wasn't selected. However, his younger brother implored the coach to give him a second chance. He did, and Sachin played much better. This summer camp got him a place at the school where Ramakant Achrekar took him under his wing and developed the champion. That imploring by his younger brother to allow Sachin into the summer camp put Tendulkar on an improved trajectory of development and led to him becoming a champion.

The question for many parents is how best to prepare for chance events. For many of our champions, their parents were keen to always have a 'Plan B' for their child in case of bad luck. This was a second career path in case they were not successful in sport for whatever reason. Mostly, this took the form of insisting that they continued education throughout their sporting development. However, the amount of focus on this compared to the core mission of becoming a sporting champion changed on a case-by-case basis; some took it very seriously, while others were less interested and put all their eggs in one basket – sport.

As far as good luck was concerned, our champions' families were flexible enough to spot unexpected opportunities and take them even if they diverted from their original plan. This could be hard for many of the parents who were planners by nature but, often, their deep knowledge of their sports meant that they were able to recognise opportunities that were too good to miss.

Throughout this book, we have looked at the many ways in which those surrounding a child have gone to incredible lengths to purposefully create a good environment for the high-quality practice essential for producing world-class sport stars. But all of this can be changed by random events, and lead to both good and bad outcomes for sporting developments. This unpredictability is one of the fascinating elements of child development.

12

Genetics

There might be thousands who aspire to be great opera singers or prima ballerinas; hundreds of thousands who would wish to play tennis like Roger Federer or swim like Michael Phelps or write like V S Naipaul. But there are millions upon millions of children and adults who play football and dream of being professional players. And Messi, scrutinised every week by those very same millions with the eye of a scientist studying an insect, is at the very top of the heap, the best player there is.[1]

Just like the millions who now look up to him, Lionel Messi grew up dreaming of being a professional footballer. Brought up in a tight-knit, football-loving family, Messi developed a passion for the sport from an early age, playing constantly with his older brothers Rodrigo and Matías and his cousins Maximiliano and Emanuel Biancucchi, both of whom became professional footballers.[2] He joined his first team aged just four, playing for local club Grandoli where his father was a coach.[3] Messi was always the smallest, as he remembers: 'I was so small, they said that when I went onto the pitch, or when I went to school, I was always the smallest of all.'[4] This forced him to create a way of playing that was different from the start; without strength to hold off defenders, Messi developed tight control, immense technical skill and the ability to turn quickly.

His ability led one of Argentina's biggest clubs, Newell's Old Boys, to sign him for their academy aged just six years old. The coaches saw Lionel as one of the greatest talents to come through the academy for many years. He could dribble with the ball as if it was attached to his foot and had a visionary ability to pick the right pass or shot. He racked up goals for his team, part of an extraordinary juniors' group that was nicknamed the 'The Machine of '87'.[5] They would often wallop competing academies by huge score lines, with Messi reportedly scoring over 500 goals for the academy.

After five years at the academy, it appeared that despite his obvious skill, there was going to be one major stumbling block to Messi succeeding at Newell's Old Boys: his size. He still cut a diminutive figure on the pitch, always the smallest and without much strength to hold off defenders. At the age of 10, other boys began to hit puberty and shoot up in height, while Messi remained very small. It became harder for Lionel to deal with the rough and tumble of the game, and the academy coaches were acutely aware that this was a problem that was only getting worse.

It became increasingly apparent that his lack of height was not just due to the usual genetic differences, and Lionel was taken to see the doctors. His parents were told that Messi had growth hormone deficiency[6], a condition caused by the pituitary gland in the brain not producing enough of the hormone needed to gain height. If left untreated, Lionel was unlikely to make it past 4 ft. 9 in. He would have no hope of becoming a professional footballer.

Fortunately, there was a treatment for the condition. By injecting growth hormone directly into one leg every night, and swapping legs every week, Messi could increase his chances of growing taller. In a bid to save his dream of becoming a professional footballer, he took the treatment, injecting himself every night. But the treatment was not without side effects.

Common impacts on children of the injections are 'headaches, muscle and joint aches, fluid retention and slippage of the hip bones'[7] – not ideal for a child athlete who depends on his agility and speed to beat opponents on the football pitch.

The greatest side effect for his parents was that the injections cost $1,500 per month. *Per month*. Money like that was simply not available to a family whose father was a factory worker and mother a part-time cleaner. They went, cap in hand, to his club Newell's Old Boys in the hope that the club would fund the treatment, given his prodigious talent. Although the club did agree to help out, the contribution was not nearly enough to cover the costs. As his father recalls: '"They said, "we will pay for the treatment, don't worry"' says Jorge, "but it was like begging, they gave me 300 pesos and never any more. If they had paid, naturally he would have stayed at Newell's."'[8]

His parents were forced to turn to the other Argentinian mega club River Plate to ask for funding in return for Messi joining their academy, but they also would not pay for the expensive treatment, given that Lionel was just 11 years old. They couldn't justify an investment of this size in someone so young. This was entirely rational from both clubs. Given that the annual CIES Football Observatory report finds that less than 1% of academy players will play professional football for a living[9], the odds were stacked against Messi even before you considered the impact of the growth hormone deficiency on his development.

The Messi family were getting desperate, and rapidly running out of money to support Lionel's treatment. They had to look further afield to try and get funding. They had relatives in Spain who resided in Catalonia, a northern region of Spain most famous for having Barcelona as its capital. Given the talent Messi had already shown for Newell's Old Boys academy, it was arranged for him to have a trial at FC Barcelona. Lionel flew over with his father, Jorge, his agent and a Barcelona contact, knowing already that this was a pivotal moment in his young life.[10] His talent had managed to get him the trial, and now it was about proving how good he could be. Messi would have just one training session to show how he could play – a lot of pressure for a 13-year-old to cope with.

Lionel impressed enough in that initial training session with his age group that Barcelona decided they wanted to see more of him. Messi would have to wait until first-team director Charly Rexach returned from visiting the Olympics to watch him play before the club would make him an offer.

Rexach watched Messi and instantly wanted to sign him. 'After two minutes, I knew', Rexach remembers.[11] He ignored Messi's size, only considering the way that the ball seemed to be stuck to his toe. Objectively, spending any kind of money on a tiny 13-year-old who needed expensive medical treatment and lived on the other side of the world would be questionable at best, insanity at worst. But Rexach was prepared to take the risk of investing in Lionel.

Rexach made a verbal offer there and then. Following that training session, Rexach moved heaven and earth to convince the club to bring him in, fighting against the facts of the situation. It took some persuasion. Not only did the club need to stump up the money to pay for Messi's treatment, they also had to find his father Jorge work, pay him an annual sum and help the whole family find somewhere to live. All of the logistics were taking time to resolve.

Negotiations slowed as Rexach tried to agree the final details with Barcelona, and the Messi family were still yet to receive anything in writing. Lionel's father became impatient, not willing to risk the opportunity to visit other Spanish clubs. They urgently called for a lunch at a tennis club in Barcelona with Rexach, where Messi's agent pronounced that they'd go elsewhere if there was no contract in place. Panicked at the thought of Messi trialling anywhere but Barca, Rexach grabbed a napkin from a plastic holder at the table. He began scribbling a contract that read: 'I, Charly Rexach, in my capacity as technical secretary for FC Barcelona, and despite the existence of some opinions against it, commit to signing Lionel Messi as long as the conditions agreed are met.' The napkin remains hidden away by Rexach to this day; a quirky artefact in the history of Lionel Messi and FC Barcelona.[12]

Unfortunately, the difficulties did not finish once Messi arrived in Barcelona. His family were deeply unhappy in Catalonia, and they desperately wanted to return home to Argentina. To compound these issues,

Messi was struggling to adjust to the lifestyle of the 'La Masia' Barcelona academy, where school, football and living were combined into one. His mother and three siblings decided to move back to Argentina after just six months in Spain, and 14-year-old Messi had to decide whether to stay with Barca or leave for home comforts. Despite struggling to fit in at his new club, he decided to stick it out as it was his best opportunity to become a footballer.[13]

Thankfully, after a few more months, Messi finally became accustomed to the lifestyle of the La Masia academy. Once settled, he quickly worked his way through the junior teams, subsequently playing for Barcelona B the feeder team for the senior squad, aged 16. At this age he was invited to train with the first-team squad as support while many first-team players were on international duty. He made a big impact.

'Messi was only 16, but he destroyed us all in a training session', French winger Ludovic Giuly explained in an interview with *Sport.*

> They were kicking him all over the place to avoid being ridiculed by this kid, but he didn't say anything. He just got up and kept on playing. Every play he made was dangerous. It was incredible. He would dribble past four players and score a goal. Even the team's starting centre-backs were nervous. They would go in hard on him, but he took it in. He was an alien. He killed us all.[14]

After this explosive initial introduction, he began training weekly with the first team as well as playing for the reserves. It wasn't long before star player Ronaldinho claimed that Messi would one day be better than him.

After making such an impression in training, players began asking the manager for Messi to be promoted to the first team permanently. Given Ronaldinho played on the left wing, manager Frank Rijkaard asked Messi to play out of position on the right wing. This situation forced by circumstance was vital to Messi's career. The right wing became Messi's position, and he learned to

cut inside onto his deadly left foot, one of the defining characteristics of his playing career.

Messi made his competitive debut in the 2004–05 season in a league game against Espanyol, coming on in the 82nd minute. At 17 years, 3 months and 22 days old, he was at the time the youngest player to represent Barcelona in an official competition.[15] He played only 77 minutes in nine matches for the first team that season, including his debut in the UEFA Champions League against Shakhtar Donetsk.

The following season he broke into the first team, and the rest is history. With Barcelona, Messi has won nine La Liga titles, four UEFA Champions League titles, and six Copas del Rey. Individually, he has received a record equalling five Ballon d'Or awards and three European Golden Boots, along with the widespread acknowledgement that he is one of the best players ever to play the beautiful game. It is perhaps his style that will be remembered even more than the awards and trophies – his ability to glide past players and finish with the perfect shot or pass has never before been seen on a football pitch. He is one of a kind.

Along with fellow academy graduates Xavi, Iniesta, Busquets and Pique, under the tutelage of Pep Guardiola, Messi was part of a team that developed a whole new style of football at Barcelona nicknamed 'tiki-taka'. It involved keeping possession, moving the ball quickly with short passes, and depending primarily on their technical skill rather than physical ability.[16] It led to world domination in club football. Many of the players in the team were small with great agility, bucking the trend of tall, physically tough players that was pervasive at the time. Messi was the cornerstone of the team, the one who could turn the endless passing into sudden bursts of action to open the deadlock when needed.

Routinely, teams resort to roughing up Messi as they simply cannot match him on the pitch. He is only 5 ft. 9 in. tall and is still a slender build at around 10 st. They niggle at him off the ball, kicking and nudging him. The minute he receives it, they try to make sure that they win the ball or cause a foul and prevent him from dribbling at all costs. When defenders swing a clumsy leg to bring him down for a free kick, for Messi it must bring back memories of playing during his childhood. The big kids have always kicked him and tried to bring him to the ground, and it's the same today. His whole game is shaped around how best to overcome these challenges.

Messi could not be further from what is considered the perfect football build. Just take a look at his arch rival, Cristiano Ronaldo, for an example of physical football perfection. He stands at 6 ft. 1 in. tall,[17] all lean muscle and toned physique. He has pace to burn, the most crucial attribute for footballers, alongside great strength, agility and jumping ability. Ronaldo has religiously refined his genetic advantages to build a physicality which has subsequently formed an unquestionable part of his success on the pitch.

In comparison, Messi, is considerably disadvantaged in terms of genetics. His size made it unlikely that he would make it in the professional game at all, unable to cope with the athletic demands of football. Many clubs had this mindset when looking at talent in their academies – with stories of kids being told they were not big enough to be professional footballers.[18] That was until Messi changed the mindset of what was possible.

What makes Messi one of the best players ever to play football is his technical ability. This was so impressive that FC Barcelona could overlook his physical deficiencies. His dribbling with the ball is genuinely ground-breaking; no one else has managed to exhibit such tight control both at high speed and while changing direction. He glides past players with an impossible grace and fluidity. When they do manage to catch up with him, he is able to pass and shoot with great vision, even from tight spaces.

In fact, it was not just despite his physical deficiencies that Messi became successful – it was arguably because of them. It was his lack of genetic suitability for football that led him to create a style that would revolutionise the game. It was because of his constraints that Messi was forced to play a different style that, ultimately, proved to be successful. At first, this seems entirely counter-intuitive: that Messi's lack of genetic gifts as a child led to him becoming one of the best players in the world. But in fact, it is something that we can look at more widely amongst our champions; for many, their lack of genetic compatibility to the conventional way of playing their sport contributed to their success.

For example, Serena Williams is not the usual build for a tennis player, with a powerful physique rather than the slender body type of many of the world's best. She used this to develop a new style of hitting with her father that was better than the rest of the competition. Similarly,

THE MAKING OF CHAMPIONS

Usain Bolt was too tall to be a 100 m sprinter, critics stating that he would not be able to get out of the blocks quickly enough to run races. His success has shown that different body types can in fact win sprint races.

The opening quote to this chapter described how it is Messi more than any other athlete in the world that kids want to emulate. Why is it that millions of children want to emulate Messi, and footballers in general, more than any other champion? There is a multitude of reasons, but one of the elements that makes football so special is the mix of physical and technical ability it requires.

In fact, we can look at all sports by the extent to which they require physical or technical abilities.

There is a spectrum between the two; all competitive sports require a mixture of both, but in different quantities. For example, archery is a prime example of an extremely technical sport. It requires little physical ability (the oldest medal winner in the Olympics in an archery event was Samuel Duvall aged 68[19]), but technical skill is everything in determining the difference between success and failure. At the other end of the spectrum, there are sports that depend primarily on physicality. A classic example of a sport towards the physicality end of the spectrum is rowing. The rowing motion is simple to repeat and can be learned quickly. Of course, this technique will be refined over time, but the vast majority of the advantage between rowing crews is a combination of power and endurance.

Meanwhile, football is an example of a sport that lies almost perfectly in the middle between physicality and technical ability. Footballers require a complex blend of stamina, strength, speed and agility in the physical department, with players showing a wide variety of strengths across these four metrics. On top of this is the layer of technical ability, and again this varies greatly by player and across a range of different types (tackling, passing, shooting, heading, etc.). Debates rage amongst fans of every club about the various merits of each player, because the sport has so many ways of winning and so many ways that a player can be valuable. Messi provides a nice illustration of how technical and physical attributes can play off against each other in football. As Lionel grew up, he was able to overcome his lack of physicality with immense technical skill.

It would seem likely that those sports on the physicality end of the spectrum would be more influenced by genetics – certain inherent natural factors such as endurance, speed or power would help considerably in the quest for victory. Meanwhile, technical sport success would instead be more down to training as skill acquisition would explain the majority of any differences.

This assumes that physical attributes are genetic, while mental attributes are not. Academic studies broadly back this theory up. Studies of twins compare those who are almost genetically identical and therefore highlight the environmental impact on height as well as other measures. These studies have shown that physical attributes (such as speed and height) are significantly driven by genetics. For example, according to *Scientific American*, height difference in children is estimated to be 60-80 per cent explainable by genetics, the rest being environmental factors (primarily diet).[20] Similarly, we can explain the natural speed and endurance of young children by the composition of fast- and slow twitch muscle fibres, which is largely determined by genes.[21] However, no attribute is 100 per cent genetic; all are influenced to some extent by the environment.

Studies comparing whether genetic or environmental factors influence mental attributes of children have also been undertaken. In general, for mental attributes, the variation amongst children tends to be explained a lot less by genetics, and more by environment. IQ variation in children is thought to be between 20–40 per cent explainable by genetics (this increases with age).[22] The big five personality traits (extraversion, agreeableness, openness, conscientiousness and neuroticism) are thought to be around 40–60 per cent explainable by genetics, according to a study published in *Nature*.[23] Therefore, we can say that genetics are likely to impact sports that depend on physical attributes more than mental attributes.

If genes are vital to sports requiring physicality, this inevitably begs the question, could we take athletes with the right genes but no background in a physical sport and make them into champions? This was always a thought exercise, until UK sport conducted this experiment themselves. The 'Sporting Giants' programme was unveiled with great fanfare back in February 2007 on behalf of the governing body. The aim was simple: find those with the height and size that gave them the potential to be champions in physicality-driven sports – rowing, handball and volleyball – and fast-track them into training for these sports at an elite level, targeting the London 2012 Games.[24]

Those applying to the program had to be a minimum of 6 ft. 3 in. for men and 5 ft. 11 in. for women, have an athletic background and be between 16 and 25[25]. Very few other 'open application' versions of these programmes into elite sport have existed before with such a focus on genetic selection. Overall, 4,800 applications were received for the scheme, 3,854 of which met the eligibility criteria.[26] It shows how much interest there was in the programme that almost 1,000 people didn't match the criteria but still tried to get onto the programme targeted GB's home Olympics.

Fast-forward five years to the results, and what was the success rate? Ten participants in the scheme became members of Team GB at the 2012 London Olympic Games; although it is important to note that six of these were involved in the first-ever GB handball team put together for the Games specifically, which did not require qualification, and therefore the competition was considerably lower. All had fairly nondescript performances, except for one: Helen Glover. Glover won her gold at London 2012 in rowing, competing in the women's coxless pair. She also went on to defend her title in Rio four years later.

Before the Sporting Giants programme, Glover had been far from a sporting novice. At high school, she was one of the best athletes, as her PE teacher remembers:

> She always had this phenomenal all-round talent, totally committed and totally reliable. You knew if you had Helen in any team you were safe. She took part in everything. She excelled in hockey and cross country. Helen was so hardworking and so coachable. If you asked her to do something, she would do it.[27]

Aged 16, Helen won a scholarship for her running and hockey talents to Millfield School in Cornwall. She competed in cross country running internationally for England (winning a junior international gold in the process). Alongside this, she competed in tennis, swimming and hockey for her county. It was in hockey that she focused most of her attention, captaining the county team and making it into the England Satellite squad – one step away from the national team.

Aged 18, Helen headed off to university with the aim of becoming a PE teacher. She graduated from Cardiff University, playing on sports teams along the way, and was preparing to continue her studies at University College Plymouth when her mum suggested she applied to the Sporting Giants programme.

She sent off her application and was duly invited to the induction session. The competitive drive in Helen was ignited by the selection process. "'They tested 4,500 of us in groups of 200 at a time," she said. "I remember sitting in a room in Bisham Abbey and someone saying: "A gold medallist in 2012 could be sat in this room. Look around you." I thought: "Right, I'm going to make that me." It was quite surreal."'[28]

The induction event should have been the end of the story for Helen. She is actually only 5 ft. 10 in., one inch shorter than the eligibility criteria, and stood on her tiptoes during her measurement at the induction event. Luckily, the coaches did not notice and she slipped through into the programme.

Glover had always been strong-willed, and the once-in-a-lifetime opportunity of competing in her home nation's Olympic Games ignited the burning drive inside her. After successfully making it through the induction session, in July 2008 she was placed on GB Rowing Team's 'Start' programme at Minerva Bath Rowing Club in Bath.[29] She transferred her studies to Bath and began concentrating on this opportunity. She quickly made an impression – her trainability and competitiveness leading her to make significant improvements compared to others on the program. She placed fourth at the British Indoor Rowing Championships just three months later.

In February 2010, Glover gave up her teaching job and lived with no income while focusing exclusively on training for the national team selection trials. That year she achieved her goal and took a huge step forward towards 2012, finishing fifth at the GB trials, winning a place on the team and gaining lottery funding.

She was paired with Heather Stanning in the women's coxless pair. The pair improved so quickly together that, by November of that year, they won a silver medal at the World Rowing Championships, finishing three seconds behind the winners.

Glover and her teammate finished second in the following year's World Rowing Championships in Slovenia, now just 0.1 seconds behind the winning New Zealand crew. This was despite both getting a stomach bug when they arrived in Slovenia. Their coach, Robin Williams, described it as 'a gold medal performance without getting the gold medal'.

In 2012, Glover and Stanning again won the coxless pair event at the GB Rowing Team selection trials. They went on to complete a clean sweep of all three events of the World Rowing Cup, looking unbeatable. It all but guaranteed them what they had been longing for since 2008 – to compete in the 2012 Olympic Games. Their dreams came true with selection.

The pair did not fail to disappoint on the biggest stage of all. In the Olympics, with the whole nation watching, Helen and her partner produced when it mattered, winning a historic gold medal in the women's coxless pair at Eton Dorney. It was Team GB's first gold medal of London 2012, and the first-ever Olympic gold medal for

British women's rowing.

The UK Sporting Giants programme heralded Glover's 2012 success. Glover had no rowing training at all in her background yet managed to win two Olympic golds after being introduced to the sport via the programme. She was competing against other British rowers who had rowed their entire life, had many more hours of practice and yet she came out on top. Similarly, she beat the best in the world, who had all been competing for many more years than her. How was this possible, given what we have looked at so far about children in sport?

As we have mentioned already, rowing is towards the physicality end of the sporting spectrum. The rowing motion is not a natural one, but there is no variation in it; once you have mastered it, the marginal improvements you can make are minor. This lack of technicality meant that skill acquisition was not a significant barrier to Helen entering rowing, compared to other sports where she would have needed months or even years to gather the technical skill to compete.

It is the speed at which you can push the oar through the water, driven by the power you can exert, over the course of the entire race that is the difference between success and failure in rowing. Long 'levers', i.e. arms and legs, are crucial for this and is the main reason why there are very few short rowers at the elite level.

These are the genetic requirements to compete in the sport. Glover had the physique required.

Given that she had the genetic requirements, and there was little technical skill to learn, what differentiated Glover from those who were already rowing? In fact, her childhood may have had more influence on her success than immediately apparent. She had been a high-quality hockey player as well as competing in cross-country running, swimming and tennis. This helped develop two specific attributes of rowers. First, she had a basic level of endurance that is difficult to replicate. Years of competing in these sports at a high level, which had continued throughout university, created a basic level of fitness that rowing coaches could work with. Playing in team sports such as hockey also helped Glover in terms of knowing how to work in a team, vital to any rowing crew.

But more importantly than either of those factors is the mentality she brought. Glover already had the Champion Mindset when she arrived at her trial day. By her own admission, she was strong-willed and focused when it came to sport. Her first experience at Bisham Abbey showed how a goal could motivate her to be extremely competitive. As mentioned even by her high school coaches, Helen was extremely trainable and coaches enjoyed working with her. This connects to the mental attributes we see in all of the athletes who became champions – competitiveness, ability to overcome failures and a deep passion for sport as her long-term motivation. She brought this Champion Mindset to the trials and the subsequent training groups, excelling to become one of the best female rowers in Team GB.

Over 3,000 entrants met the eligibility criteria of the Sporting Giants programme, yet there was only one medallist. For those who believe that genetic talent is the differentiator, there would be an expectation that the most physically gifted athletes would have been successful in representing GB at the Olympics and winning medals. In fact, it was the one who didn't meet the eligibility criteria, but had the right mentality, who was able to make it to the podium.

Genetics can be an obstacle to being a sporting champion as a child. If you do not have the physical attributes required for some sports, particularly those that depend more on physicality than technical skill, there is little opportunity for success. But in others, which are more focused on skill acquisition, there will always be opportunities. Lionel Messi could not have been a rower, but he could (just about) be a footballer – and in fact benefited from his lack of physical attributes. In all cases of these sporting champions, the mentality developed during childhood, created mainly by the environment, is the differentiator rather than genes.

13

The Nearly Ones

The Heisman Trophy is awarded at the end of each season to the most outstanding player in college football in the United States. It is a coveted award that kids right across the United States, from those running around their front yards to those representing colleges in front of packed-out stadiums, dream of winning – for many, on a par with playing in the NFL. According to the Heisman Trophy Trust: 'The Heisman Memorial Trophy annually recognizes the outstanding college football player whose performance best exhibits the pursuit of excellence with integrity. The winners of the trophy epitomise great ability combined with diligence, perseverance, and hard work.'[1] It is voted for primarily by sports journalists (870 votes) with fans (1 vote) and previous Heisman winners (57 votes)[2] also getting a say in who takes the trophy home.

The Heisman is handed out just before the postseason playoffs begin in December. The top college athletes are already big stars, perhaps even as big as NFL headline names. But the Heisman elevates them to another level and ensures they will never be forgotten in American football folklore. The collection of athletes who have won the Heisman have varied stories of how they got there, and equally varied outcomes of what happened to them afterwards.

From the perspective of *The Making of Champions*, this gives us a unique opportunity. The Heisman sits at the apex where amateurs are becoming professionals, at the end of their childhoods before they become pros. It determines the single best American Football junior in the country. We can use this to help look at how this junior success converted into professional accomplishment.

Even amongst this rarefied group of successful college athletes, 1962 winner Terry Baker stands out from the rest. He is perhaps one of the best college athletes of all time, his American football skills being the jewel in his crown. In 1962, Baker steered Oregon State Beavers to a state championship as an exceptional all-round quarterback. Not content with being the best footballer in the country, he led the Oregon State basketball team to the 'Final Four', the national semi-finals – the only athlete ever to both win the Heisman Trophy and appear in the 'Final Four'.[3] He is revered in Oregon where his number 11 jersey is permanently retired.

Just after receiving the Heisman Trophy, Baker was featured on the cover of Sports Illustrated.[4] The picture is a standard portrait, his body facing slightly off camera, hands together in a startlingly similar pose to a yearbook entry. Wearing a sensible black V-neck jumper, shirt and dark blue tie, Terry stares into the camera looking completely self-assured. He looks more like a successful businessman rather than a recent college graduate. He was featured on the cover having been awarded the magazine's Sportsman of the Year accolade, an award that has also been presented to the likes of Muhammad Ali, Michael Jordan and Tiger Woods.[5] In the moment captured in this photo, Baker seems to have the world at his feet.

Baker's sporting talent began to get noticed while at Jefferson High School. Even then, his future as an athlete was full of promise – regardless of what sport he went into. In football, he settled into the role of quarterback, driving the team forward with his elegant passing game. Baker was also one of the best talents on both the basketball and baseball teams. He was described by his coach as a 'great competitor' who could 'visualise things that other players can't'.[6]

His brother, Gary, remembers the ferocity with which Terry used to work at his sports:

> He didn't just go over there to Peninsula Park for exercise, you know. He would work on one specific thing every weekend. He'd master it and then he'd go on to something else. He actually used to have a system worked out. He would try to master one thing a week. At the end of the year he would have mastered 52 things. Take his left-handed hook shot. He'd work on it the entire weekend. He'd get it down good, and then he'd go on to something else.[7]

He was undergoing a practice regimen reminiscent of our other champions, driven to improve through Deliberate Practice. Success followed.

Baker was outstanding at all his sports. In his senior year at Jefferson High, he was selected in the all-state teams across the United States' big three sports: football, basketball and baseball – an astonishing feat. Aside from individual accolades, he also guided the school to win the city title in all three sports, the state title in two. He was one of the most outstanding athletes in the country.

As a result, Terry was showered with offers from colleges desperate to secure his signature across all three sports. He eventually plumped for Oregon State on a basketball scholarship, where his brother was studying.

On arrival at Oregon State, Baker decided to focus on basketball and not try out for the football team in his freshman year. He didn't believe his finesse passing game would be well suited to the way that the Oregon State Beavers football team played at the time. He immediately settled in to be a key player in Oregon's basketball team, becoming their highest scorer with an average of 17.8 points per game. He also played a quarterback-style role in the team, directing and leading the team from the guard position.

In the spring of his freshman year, Baker reversed his decision and decided to try out for the Oregon State Beavers football team for the upcoming season. He was thought to be a no-hoper by competing freshmen and coaches alike. Although he had been successful at high school level, his upper body 'looked like a literary student', according to Coach Prothro. They felt he would not be strong enough to hold his own in the college game.

Baker's ability quickly changed the coaches' minds. In his sophomore (second) year, he broke into the team and began to appear regularly. Terry was alternated with a well-proven senior at halfback, both passing and carrying the ball – a surprise for an individual whose game up to that point had been successful solely due to his passing ability. Despite his game time being half of many competitors, Terry managed to amass record-breaking offense figures; most notably setting a new Oregon State record for total offense yards. These yards were split equally amongst running and passing, despite Baker's lack of experience in the former. His fearlessness in throwing himself over the gain line more than compensated for his slender physique.

Given this success, Coach Prothro decided to change the team's shape the following season to better suit Baker's talent. It was not an instant success, with Oregon having a disappointing season of five wins and five losses. Part of the issue was that Baker was not allowed to run due to no other quarterback being in the squad. This meant he couldn't mix up his game as he had done the previous year to such great effect. However, he still managed to be rated the 11th best player in the country – not bad for a sophomore.

It was in his senior season that Baker took his success to the next level. In the 1962 season, he threw for a total of 1,738 yards and ran for another 538, absolutely decimating the competition to have the most offensive yards of any college player in the country. Baker and his coach had finally hit on the formula; most of the plays would be designed so that Terry rolled out the pocket, where he could either run or pass. The uncertainty over what Baker would do created opportunities, and Baker excelled in the split-second decision-making that was vital in making this tactic a success.

The team flourished, winning their first six games and going on to gain a national ranking. Entering the playoffs, positivity was high that Oregon State could produce something special. The team progressed to the semi-final. In a match against Colorado State, Baker produced a heroic display to accumulate 389 total offensive yards and help the team to a three-point win, sending the Oregon State Beavers to the Liberty Bowl final. It was the first state bowl game for the Beavers in five years. They went in as favourites against the Villanova Wildcats.

An open, attacking game was expected. But unfortunately, the weather ensured that this did not happen. Cold weather had frozen the pitch, creating a new challenge for both teams as attacking play became extremely difficult. The game was played at a crawling pace and was inevitably going to be decided by one or two scores. In the end, it was decided by a single play that is still recounted by those who remember it as one of the best they have ever seen.

The score was 0–0 with less than 10 minutes left. Oregon had possession one yard away from their own in-goal area. They snapped the ball to Baker. He stepped back, in his own touchdown area, peeling towards the sideline as he looked for an out pass. Despite furious blocking by his team, two Wildcards defenders managed to get through. It seemed definite that they would tackle him and earn Villanova a crucial two points. But Baker somehow slipped these tackles, avoided another and ran the entire length of the field for a 99-yard touchdown.[8] It proved the only score of the game and won Oregon their first title since 1942. Baker recalls: 'The 99-yard run has taken on a life of its own. It's one of the few records that will never be broken.'[9]

Not only was Baker setting the college football world alight, but incredibly he was also one of the best college basketball players too. In the same 1962 season, Baker captained the basketball team to the semi-finals of the Division 1 basketball tournament, known in the United States as the 'Final Four'.[10] His ability to lead, direct and drive the team forwards made them one of the most formidable teams in the country.

Plaudits and awards rained down on him. Baker was awarded the Heisman Trophy and was also a unanimous all-American in both football and basketball. He swept the board with awards, winning everything on offer to a college athlete. He was a guest of honour at the Army v Navy game, meeting President Kennedy who knew him by name.[11] The future seemed bright and promising for a professional career.

The Los Angeles Rams' scouting report gave Baker the highest rating there is for a college prospect. One of their scouts wrote:

> An amazing athlete, excellent passer either short or long. Throws well under pressure, concentrating on the receiver rather than the rush. A tremendous runner whose speed has improved with his passing each year. Very intelligent, very good signal-caller and an outstanding leader.[12]

After graduating, Baker was made offers by baseball, basketball and football teams. He chose football and was selected as first pick by the Los Angeles Rams in the 1963 NFL Draft. Of course, he was now a professional rather than an amateur – the Rams signed him to an annual salary of $25,000 and gave him a $15,000 bonus. 'I thought I was wealthy,' Baker said.[13] He was earning for the first time in his life, and the future seemed set for Baker to become one of the NFL's biggest names after a stellar junior career playing at the highest possible level.

Baker was woken abruptly from his perfect ascent to stardom once he arrived in LA. His professional career was about to get off to an appalling start at the Rams. He remembers his first experience after being drafted:

> The Rams were so unorganized when I joined them that the coaches didn't know what was going on. I started my first game, and I was no more prepared to do that than the man in the moon. I threw three interceptions, and I think [Rams head coach] Harland Svare lost confidence in me right there. I didn't have a strong arm, and it soon got sore because the amount of passing one had to do in the pro game was more than I could take.[14]

Rams head coach Harland Svare sent Baker to a psychiatrist straight after his first game due to the poor performance. Incredibly, it was determined by the psychiatrist that 'Baker's arm hates Harland'.[15] It was determined his arm hated the coach and that this was unrecoverable; something that didn't bode well for Baker's career as quarterback with the Rams. After being on top of the world, it seemed like Baker's career was suddenly entering a downward spiral. He was moved to halfback, where his lack of out-and-out speed at the professional level and a series of niggling injuries meant he never made an impression.

Head coach Svare also remembers Baker's potential, but that it was his arm that let him down: 'He was a great athlete and a tremendous person. He had great command out there. He was a tremendous field general and very intelligent. He did everything he was supposed to do, except he didn't have an arm.'[16]

In total, during three seasons, Baker would finish his NFL career with the following statistics: 18 games, 1 touchdown, 4 Interceptions, 364 yards total.[17] He had earned better stats in a single game for Oregon.

After leaving the LA Rams, Baker moved to Canada in

the hope of getting a starter quarterback berth. He played a single season for the Edmonton Eskimos, who he led to the Bowl game with a string of great performances, before leaving football in 1966 to become a lawyer.

Four years earlier, Baker had won the Heisman Trophy, been a consensus all-American in football and basketball and won Sports Illustrated Sportsman of the Year. Yet, aged just 25, he was finished playing football. Moving to the professionals had been a step too far for Baker. Even someone with the pedigree of a Heisman winner was not good enough to make it in the professional game. Even someone who had the perfect junior career was still a 'nearly one', one of a long list of those who didn't manage to succeed in the NFL. The small number of starting positions in the NFL, and the popularity of the sport, means there is a huge number who don't quite make it.

Although most have translated Heisman success into a good NFL career, there are others who have had faltered in the professional ranks following successful college years. There are few who have polarised opinion amongst American football fans quite like Heisman winner Tim Tebow. Some see him as the salt-of-the-earth all-American hero that everyone wants to be: a talented, hard-working, deeply Christian leader of men who can pull off the impossible when it is needed most. Others see him as an overhyped, self-righteous and ultimately average quarterback. It was his personality, combined with disagreements over his ability, that means he is a particularly interesting case of a Heisman winner who never quite made it as a starter in the NFL.

Tim Tebow is possibly one of the most religious athletes in the world, and his upbringing is the reason. His parents, Robert and Elaine, met at the University of

Florida. After 14 years of marriage, they moved to the Philippines with their young family to be Baptist missionaries. It was in the Philippines that they had Timothy Richard Tebow, their fifth child.[18]

Tim spent his whole childhood being home schooled by his parents. This was part of a wider trend of devout Christian families deciding to home school their children in order to ensure they were instilled with strong Christian values.[19] Up until 1996, home schooled kids were not allowed to take part in high-school sports.[20] This changed in Florida just in time for Tim, who got the opportunity to play the game he loved: American football.

He began to attract attention for his talents as early as his junior year of high school. Tebow was known for having one of the best all-round games in the country for his age; the killer ability to both pass and run that created uncertainty for opposition defences. This was combined with an unparalleled competitiveness and great leadership qualities that were unusual for someone of his age.

During his senior year, Tebow led the Nease Panthers to a state title, earned All-State honours, was named Florida's Mr Football and was a Parade magazine high-school all-American.[21] With his exceptional football talent, unusual background and fiercely competitive nature, he was unique and drew attention for this.

Following his high-school career, Tebow decided to stay close to home and attend the University of Florida on a scholarship, subsequently playing for the Gators. He started as second-string quarterback for the 2006 season but was used regularly. In particular, the coach utilised his running ability, and he finished his first season with the second most rushing yards for the Gators. Tebow was already building a healthy reputation for converting on crucial plays too.

In the 2007 season, Tebow got his chance as starting quarterback. The polarisation of opinion that would define his career had already started – questions over his passing ability were weighed against his obvious leadership qualities as quarterback. But he had an incredible season, quashing many doubters. By the end of the campaign, he had the most touchdowns ever for a South-eastern Conference season (55), and the most rushing touchdowns (20). This won him the Heisman, and his popularity grew across the United States, partially due to his faith-driven motivations.

Although 2008 saw Tebow taking a joint role at quarterback, it saw him leading a team performance that would take the Gators to the national championships. A 12–1 record gave them the #2 ranking in the country and sent them to the 2009 BCS National Championships game against Oklahoma. It was a showdown for Tebow against Sam Bradford, the quarterback who took the Heisman from him that year. The final was held in front of a Miami Dolphin stadium record crowd of 78,468.

After a tense encounter, the game entered the final five minutes with Florida leading 17–14. As the Gators marched down the pitch, a run by Tebow edged them closer: just four yards away from the end zone. On the next play, Tebow received the ball at quarterback. He ran forward as if to make a dash for the line, before leaping up in the air and throwing a short pass to receiver Nelson in a play that would win the game. The stadium erupted: Tebow had done it again.

It was the final act of a stunning college career which

Tebow finished with a slew of records: 5 National Collegiate Athletic Association (NCAA), 14 South-eastern Conference and 28 University of Florida statistical records. It was now time for Tebow to progress to the pros, Heisman in tow. Despite his college success, Tebow's NFL potential was much discussed in the 2010 draft.

For football fans, Tebow's style as a quarterback was still a cause for debate. A lack of quality fundamentals meant little fluidity in his style. His passing technique was poor compared to other hot prospects in the draft. This lack of passing basics may have led to the development of his unconventional style which depended on his powerful physique and running ability. It was unclear if this new style was the sign of a revolutionary new type of quarterback or simply that Tebow was not as good as other prospects. His high-school and college success could not be argued with and, importantly, it highlighted the mental side of the game in which Tebow excelled. He had developed an incredible ability to pull off great plays at crucial moments that was always going to be attractive to NFL teams – although perhaps less so than it appealed to fans.

He was selected as the 25th pick in the first round of the 2010 draft for the Denver Broncos. Such was his popularity that he set an NFL Draft record for jersey sales and continued to have the top-selling jersey through the 2010 season.[22]

Tebow had a stuttering start to his career with the Broncos. Despite some good moments, Tebow failed to convince and was used sparingly as a back-up in the last six games of the season. Like Baker, he was given limited game time to prove his worth, with just one start in this first season, a 39–23 defeat to the Oakland Raiders.

Better opportunities came his way in the 2011 season. After a poor start to the campaign, in their fifth game of the year, Tebow replaced starting quarterback Randy Orton at half-time. After narrowing a 16-point deficit to 5 points by the close, Tebow earned himself a start against the Miami Dolphins. Tebow led the team to an 18–15 victory in overtime, and the good feeling returned to the Broncos. Reminiscent of the heroics of Tebow's performances in college, what followed was a rush of come-from-behind victories.

The Broncos did enough to make it into the postseason. Tebow had been waiting for this chance his entire life; a starting quarterback in a playoff game. He threw for a career-high 316 yards and two touchdowns, but still the game went to overtime at 23 apiece. On the very first play of overtime, in a classic Tebow moment, he threw an 80-yard touchdown to win the game. Once again, the United States couldn't get enough of him.

In the next game of the playoffs, Tebow was brought back down to earth as the Broncos were knocked out. He completed just 9 of 26 passes and took five sacks in a 45–10 defeat at the hands of the New England Patriots. Despite the relative success of the team by making the playoffs, Tebow finished with the lowest passing completion rate of any player in the NFL. This again raised questions over his ability to be a starting quarterback in the professional game.

After the season, Tebow was traded to the New York Jets as a result of star Peyton Manning being signed by the Broncos as a free agent. Tebow's NFL career would never recover. The Jets struggled throughout the season, but the coaches would not listen to the cries for Tebow to be thrown in instead of the inconsistent quarterback Mark Sanchez. Tebow threw only 8 passes and ran 32 times in his single season with the Jets.

Tebow was released and signed for the following season by the New England Patriots. Despite appearing in preseason, he didn't manage to make the roster cut and was released. He entered broadcasting while still actively looking for his next NFL opportunity, taking advantage of his popularity to stay in the public consciousness. The next year followed a similar disappointment, as he competed in preseason for a berth as third string quarterback at the Philadelphia Eagles. Again, he failed to make the cut. He is the only quarterback aged under 30 in NFL history to win a playoff game and then never start another NFL game.

In early 2016, he finally dropped his NFL dream and decided to turn his hand to baseball. He invited the media, who arrived in their dozens, to an open training session. He has since signed a minor-league contract with the New York Mets and is looking to rebuild his career in one of the United States' other darling sports – but the road ahead looks long and winding if he is ever going to achieve success in Major League Baseball.

Both Baker and Tebow had the perfect junior careers to set them up for the NFL. First of all, they both developed the Champion Mindset in bucketloads. They were known for their intensely competitive nature, being great at responding to failure and having deep passion for the game. On top of that, they displayed a formidable work ethic and ability to practice well. Their environment was also suitable for success; they grew up playing American football in the nation that worships the sport, having a clear institutional path that guides talent from high school through to the professional game with high-quality practice and coaching.

After being standout performers at high school, they landed at the right college teams who nurtured them and built teams to take advantage of their talents. Despite some initial difficulties, they rose to the challenge and both showed the killer instinct to produce their best at the critical moments: Baker running for a decisive 99-yard touchdown in Oregon's Bowl game and Tebow throwing a 4-yard touchdown pass to win the national championships for Florida. They were both awarded the Heisman for their performances.

However, despite having all the attributes of champions, they both failed in the NFL. Remember, these were the best athletes at college level by the most recognised standard, yet neither managed to nail down a starting position in a franchise for an entire season. Baker had a disappointing career, managing only a handful of appearances for the LA Rams, while Tebow's promise amounted to one playoff victory, and never maintaining a quarterback starting berth in the NFL. Why were these talented juniors unable to carve out even average careers in the NFL?

Amongst all the discussion in *The Making of Champions* so far, there is one point that is easy to overlook: there can only be one champion, and this inevitably means there must be many, many 'nearly ones'. Throughout this book, we have shown 'survivorship bias', only presenting the stories of those who become champions in their sports. However, these are the rarities. Many, many more do not make it. Baker and Tebow are two examples of athletes who got very close to the top but did not manage to succeed at an elite level. The sheer weight of numbers of individuals competing for NFL berths means the competition is cut-throat and, even with the right attributes, environment and opportunities, sometimes that's still not enough. Due to the high media attention on the winners, we tend to focus on the successful athletes rather than the stories of those who do not make it.

There are just over 1,696 athletes in the NFL. About 1.23 million start playing American football in the United States between the ages of 6 and 12.[23] The NCAA estimated 1.06 million play in high school, before 73,063 make it through to college teams.[24] Of these, 1.9 per cent make it to the pros and those fabled 1,696 places in the NFL – about 0.013 per cent of those who initially start playing the game. The odds are always stacked against you making it to the top.

If you do make it, the benefits are huge. On top of the fame and glory, Forbes estimates that the average NFL salary in 2016 was $2.1 million per year, without considering other endorsements and incomes. The same news source predicts the highest earning player in 2017 was quarterback Cam Newton, who racked up staggering total yearly earnings of $53.1 million.[25] A few years in the NFL can provide enough money, if managed correctly, to support a family for a lifetime. It is still seen as a rare way out of poverty for the poorest in the United States. As a result, they pin all their hopes on becoming the next Cam Newton – despite the miniscule odds of making it to the top.

What is left afterwards if you don't make it? Thousands of hours sunk into a sport that, at best, will be continued as a hobby, at worst will not be able to be enjoyed again. There will also be the need to find a new career path. Unlike many, Baker was able to become a lawyer. This was a result of achieving good grades while studying at Oregon which allowed him to go to law school. Tebow achieved enough popularity during his college days to sustain a career in commentary before entering another sport. But for many athletes, the opportunities are much sparser. In an effort to prepare kids for a potential future without sport, the United States has taken a lead by only offering sport advancement through the school system provided kids obtain some form of academic achievement.

Of course, there are many positives to playing sport outside of money, fame and glory. Besides the obvious physical health benefits, the friendships and the memories can be some of the highlights of people's lives. It can build the mental attributes that are often related to success across a range of different fields. The effect on well-being should also not be underestimated. Sport is so often a cornerstone of living a positive healthy life. This is something that should not be forgotten when thinking about the pursuit of greatness through sport, and the odds stacked against making it to the top level.

It is this curious paradox that brings a certain drama to the story of kids attempting to become one of the best in the world at sport. Those who dedicate the most time are most likely to be successful – yet they are also those who have the most to lose. All the evidence suggests that a more balanced life will not lead to being a champion – the amount of dedication to practice and competition required for youngsters to succeed nowadays is all-consuming – so, by dedicating so much, future opportunities outside sport diminish. It is why all victories are tinged with relief.

When talking about childhood sport, it would be irresponsible not to talk about the thousands of 'nearly ones'. There are many more of them than the few that make it to the top. We must consider that the end goal of sporting success may be desirable, but the costs of committing to a sport but not achieving could also be great.

14

Conclusion

We began *The Making of Champions* by looking at four astonishing moments in sporting history: Bolt obliterating the 100 m world record in Beijing; Nadia Comăneci producing the first-ever perfect 10 routine in Montreal; Phelps' come-from-behind victory on his way to a record-breaking eight golds; and Ali defeating Foreman in the Rumble in the Jungle to reclaim his title as Heavyweight Champion of the World. Throughout this book, we have delved deeper into the stories of these champions (and others) to better understand how formative moments in their childhood helped them become the best athletes in the world.

So, how do children become sporting champions? At the very heart of all of their successes, it is their mindset, developed during childhood, that is the differentiator. Two main attributes form this mindset. First, all our athletes were supremely competitive, either with themselves or with others. They loved winning in all its forms, whether that was against their own personal bests or in competition against others. Although they hated losing terribly, they did not give up as many competitive children do. Our champions had incredible persistence to try again at the same sport rather than quit, regardless of the number of failures.

Our athletes combined this competitiveness with motivation that was either driven by passion for the sport or the desire for fame and glory. Interestingly, some of our champions were motivated by fame and glory from the very beginning, always seeing the financial and fame benefits of sport. As many of our champions grew up, their motivation fluctuated between these two sources, with the most common trend being passion for the sport slowly making way for the desire for fame and glory. The short-term motivator of competitiveness drove these children to practise and compete hard on a daily basis, ensuring the right intensity to improve. The long-term motivation of passion for sport/desire for fame and glory drove them on over a prolonged period and prevented burnout. We've titled this mentality the Champion Mindset.

This Champion Mindset was cultivated in our child athletes by those around them; whether it was coaches, parents, school, siblings, institutions or networks. Those who shaped the environment around these athletes had a second function too; they ensured the athletes had the opportunities to succeed in terms of access to the right resources. For different athletes, different people took a leading role in developing their mindset and creating the right opportunities. For an energetic kid from Baltimore, a coach provided the perfect individual to develop his competitiveness with himself, as well as providing the top-tier coaching needed to succeed. For two girls from Compton learning tennis, their parents were the centrepiece of their development, constantly focusing on their mentality and providing coaching on the tennis courts. For a Mumbai cricketer, school provided the springboard for development, providing the coaching as well as the cricket nets and equipment needed. For a young sprinter born in Jamaica, the strength of the institutions took care of everything from coaching to funding, while parents developed the mindset. For a young racing-car driver, networks within the sport got him the opportunity he needed to succeed. For each athlete, cultivating the right environment to develop the mentality and create opportunities for success was different.

The child athletes were developing the Champion Mindset and the right environment for success had been created; now they needed the key activity to become champions: practice, practice, practice. In this area, despite the wide variety of sports, there were striking similarities about the way that our athletes practised. Almost all of the practice undertaken in their sports was under the watchful eye of a talented coach, who was able to provide feedback and assist in planning – very little was conducted on their own. This was because coaches could help ensure the child had the practice plan to follow each day, provide encouragement and ensure the right long-term goals were being pursued. Having a talented coach who handled this meant our young athletes could focus simply on executing each practice session. We also looked at how similar the practice of our child athletes matched the Deliberate Practice methodology outlined by practice expert Dr Anders Ericsson. These athletes practised every day in ways which closely resembled the Deliberate Practice methodology, for example setting well-defined goals with a clear plan to achieve them and always working on

225

the worst parts of their performance. Finally, we finished reviewing their practice habits by considering how the quantity of practice during childhood is increasing. This is reflected at the highest level by the increasing quality of sport over time. This trend will only continue and force some difficult decisions in the future about trade-offs between practice and other aspects of a child's life.

Having developed a good understanding of how our child athletes succeeded, we also need to understand the pitfalls that they missed on their path to becoming champions. We cannot fail to ignore that, despite their careful planning, there was always an element of luck in the development of our champions. While there is a huge amount that can be done to shape an environment and prepare a child for success in sport, this only increases the probability of success; luck can always play a role in making or breaking the development of an athlete. Our champions avoided catastrophic bad luck such as career-ending injuries, and many profited from random events that helped them get the right opportunities they needed for success. The young athletes also won the genetic lottery in terms of having the right physical attributes that are the minimum requirement for competing in their sport – although, as we saw in the case of Messi, this is not the delimiting factor it was once thought. We looked at the interesting dynamic of those not fitting into the stereotypical physical build for their sports actually becoming champions as it forced them to compete in a different way. Finally, our athletes managed to become champions despite spectacularly long odds of making it, given the competitiveness in the junior ranks of sport.

We have also considered the potential downsides for youngsters seeking to become sporting champions. This was because a book that studies the childhoods of those who become sporting champions suffers from 'survivorship bias'; by focusing on those who make it, we ignore the thousands who equally strove to be the best but did not make it to the top.

Taking on the journey to becoming a sporting champion is not for the faint-hearted. The quantity of practice, the shaping of an environment for success and competing at the highest level all over the world inevitably require significant sacrifices for any child. None of our champions had what would be described as 'normal' childhoods, with many not having as much free time and play as would be expected for most children. Education often came second in importance, despite leading to a greater chance of economic prosperity compared to the sporting world. These are factors that need to be considered.

Of course, this needs to be compared to the benefits of following the sporting path. Sport promotes a healthy lifestyle, as well as teaching life skills such as a growth mentality, teamwork and work ethic that will be useful no matter what direction is followed in later life. Our champions are now hugely successful adults and are an inspiration to millions of children around the world. But, particularly with the trend of increased practice in childhood and the pressures this will put on squeezing out other activities, deciding to follow the path to being a champion is not a decision that can be made lightly.

Now we have a better understanding of how children develop into sporting champions, how do we help the next generation reach achieve sporting greatness? There are three key points for those looking to develop the stars of the future that are contrary to current popular advice on coaching.

This book began by looking at the core attribute that contributed to the champions success - the Champion Mindset. Currently, there is not enough focus on developing mental attributes in young athletes. Training and games should look to develop a burning competitiveness in athletes and should shy away from 'everyone's a winner' mentality. Developing high quality competition at every level of development is a key principle for sporting success. Secondly, managing the long-term motivation is also something coaches and parents should actively think about – whether that is the motivation for glory or passion for the sport. Actively developing these mental attributes is crucial, but currently is not a core part of the curriculum in most sport coaching institutions.

Secondly, practice being undertaken with junior athletes is often not as effective as it could be. Many of the champions reviewed in this book used practice methods closely aligned to the Deliberate Practice methodology, but this is rarely used at a junior level as a model for improvement. Looking to align better with this model will yield more efficient improvement. Our champions also managed an astonishing quantity of practice, which may be a consideration for those only practising a couple of times a week.

Finally, a more realistic view of the challenges in becoming a sporting champion need to be considered with the next generation. Given the role of luck and the huge number of children dreaming of becoming professional athletes, working on the basis of increasing the probability of success rather than aiming for guaranteed achievement is an important distinction. Understanding the likelihood of being a sporting champion, effective alternative plans in case of bad luck should be designed.

Implementing these three lessons with the next generation of athletes should help them improve their chances of becoming a sporting champion. The quality of executing these will prove the difference, something that the parents and coaches within this book excelled at.

We finished the Introduction by asking the question that gnaws away at many amateur adult athletes: could I have made it to the top? The answer is yes - if your environment during your upbringing had been primarily focussed on building a Champion Mindset. Unless you are genetically unsuited to a sport, with this mindset, a supportive environment and deliberate practice techniques defined, you would have had a good chance of becoming a world champion in your chosen sport. There is little innate characteristics of our world champions that differentiated them – instead, they had radically different upbringings that led to exceptional success in their chosen sport.

The Making of Champions is done by us, not genetics.

About the Author

Edward Lowe has had a lifelong obsession with sport and practice. After developing knowledge of a wide range of sports and studying sport psychology, he wrote *The Making of Champions* to contribute to the existing studies of how sporting success is developed.

He authored his first book 'CTFC – The Recent Years' in 2012 whilst still in high school. The book chronicled the past 10 years of Cheltenham Town Football Club through interviews with owners, players and managers. This included interviews with Sir Geoff Hurst, Alan Shearer and Jack Butland. The book sold out its print run within a year and received local press attention.

He continued to write about sport upon attendance at Oxford University to read Economics & Management, rising to be editor of Oxfords oldest student newspaper, The Cherwell.

He now works as a Technology Consulting Analyst at Accenture, living in London. He continues to write for online publications, including The Huffington Post.

Acknowledgements

There is one person I would like to thank first - Sophie Young, my long-suffering girlfriend who has put up with this book swallowing up most of my free time once work and watching Aston Villa are also considered. You continue to be amazingly supportive of all my endeavours.

During the writing process, a pivotal moment was the feedback I received on the first three chapters once they were completed. The feedback I received was invaluable, helping to improve everything from the sentence composition to the rigour of my arguments. For this I want to thank Vanessa Lowe, Josh Weekly, Akshay Chauhan, Oliver Martin, David Phippard, Wilson Hill, Jamie Miller, Will Wright, Claire Somerset and Fred Ahern.

I'd like to also acknowledge a group of writers who have inspired, moved and enthralled me with their writing on this topic. For this, I want to thank Malcolm Gladwell, Matthew Syed, Anders Ericsson and David Epstein whose books peaked my interested in this topic.

Finally, two people helped to transform this from a hobbyist project to a professional book. Thank you to Fergus Paton for your role as copy-editor and helping to significantly raise the standard of this book. Thank you also to M2Design for completing the cover design. Both are thoroughly recommended.

References

1. Prologue
[1] "Usain Bolt Wins 100m/200m Gold - Beijing 2008 Olympics", Olympics Channel, 2010 [YouTube], accessed 2018, https://www.youtube.com/watch?v=F14EaVEDyUs&t=34s
[2] "The first Olympic gymnast to score a perfect 10", BBC News, 2016, accessed 2018, http://www.bbc.co.uk/news/magazine-36826597
[3] "Swimming - Men's 100M Butterfly Final - Beijing 2008 Summer Olympic Games", Athleticsgymnastics, 2008 [YouTube], accessed 2018, https://www.youtube.com/watch?v=DNKrQBGdYW0
[4] "George Foreman vs Muhammad Ali - Oct. 30, 1974 - Entire fight - Rounds 1 - 8 & Interview", Levi Johansen, 2010 [YouTube], https://www.youtube.com/watch?v=55AasQJZzDE&t=3149s
[5] Ibid
[6] "Outliers: The Story of Success", Malcolm Gladwell, Penguin, 2009.
[7] "The role of Deliberate Practice in the Acquisition of Expert Performance", Anders Ericsson, Psychological Review p.363-406, 1993.
[8] "The Sports Gene: Talent, Practice and the Truth about Success", David Epstein, Yellow Jersey, 2014.

2. Competitiveness
[1] "Michael Jordan", Wikipedia, accessed March 2018, https://en.wikipedia.org/wiki/Michael_Jordan
[2] "2007-08 Player Survey: Height" NBA.com, accessed March 2018, http://www.nba.com/news/survey_height_2007.html
[3] Michael Jordan", Wikipedia, accessed March 2018, https://en.wikipedia.org/wiki/Michael_Jordan
[4] "Male Body Image and the Average Athlete", PsychGuides, accessed July 2018, https://www.psychguides.com/interact/male-body-image-and-the-average-athlete/
[5] "Michael Jordan: The Life" Roland Lazenby, Back Bay, 2015, p.86.
[6] Ibid, p.47
[7]"Portrait of a legend", Melissa Isaacson, ESPN.com, 2009, accessed July 2018,

http://www.espn.com/chicago/columns/story?columnist=isaacson_melissa&id=4457017

[8] "Michael Jordan: The Life" Roland Lazenby, Back Bay, 2015, p.71

[9] Ibid, p. 86

[10] "Michael Jordan", Wikipedia, accessed 2018, https://en.wikipedia.org/wiki/Michael_Jordan

[11] "Cristiano Ronaldo Coaching Euro 2016 Final (PORTUGAL vs FRANCE)", LosBlancos TV, 2016 [YouTube], accessed March 2018, https://www.youtube.com/watch?v=nW8QDNnXVlk

[12] "Ronaldo: The Obsession of Perfection", Luca Caioli, Icon Books, 2012, p.12

[13] Ibid, p.14

[14] "Cristiano Ronaldo was nicknamed 'cry baby' for his tantrums, admits former teammate", Sports Staff, The Guardian, 2017, accessed March 2018, https://www.independent.co.uk/sport/football/european/real-madrid-cristiano-ronaldo-was-nicknamed-cry-baby-for-his-tantrums-admits-former-teammate-a7653836.html

[15] "Ronaldo: The Obsession of Perfection", Luca Caioli, Icon Books, 2012, p.22

[16] Ibid, p. 22 - 23.

[17] Ibid, p. 1 – 4

3. Motivation

[1] "Paula: My Story So Far", Paula Radcliffe, Simon & Schuster UK, 2005

[2] Ibid, p.11

[3] Ibid, p.13

[4] "Picking up the pace", Patrick Barkham, The Guardian, 2008, accessed March 2018, https://www.theguardian.com/sport/2008/dec/16/paula-radcliffe

[5] "Paula Radcliffe: behind the smile, and tears, a desire to be better than great", Sean Ingle, The Guardian, 2015, accessed Jan 2018, https://www.theguardian.com/sport/2015/apr/25/paula-radcliffe-behind-the-smile-and-tears-a-desire-to-be-better-than-great

[6] "No Limits: The Will to Succeed", Michael Phelps and Alan Abrahamson, Simon & Schuster UK, 2009, p.19

[7] "Faster Than Lightning: My Story", Usain Bolt, HarperSport, 2014, p.17

[8] "Nick Kyrgios", Wikipedia, accessed March 2018, https://en.wikipedia.org/wiki/Nick_Kyrgios

[9] "Nick Kyrgios booted off ATP Tour for extended period due to Shanghai Masters capitulation", ABC News, 2016, accessed July 2018, http://www.abc.net.au/news/2016-10-17/nick-kyrgios-booted-off-atp-tour-for-extended-period/7940834

[10] "Enigmatic as ever, Nick Kyrgios makes early exit from US Open", Simon Cambers, ESPN, 2017, accessed January 2018,http://www.espn.com/tennis/story/_/id/20510205/us-open-enigmatic-ever-nick-kyrgios-questions-own-dedication-quick-exit

[11] "Muhammad Ali: His Life and Times", Thomas Hauser, Portico, 2012, p.14

[12] Ibid, p.19

[13] Ibid, p.20

[14] Ibid, p.16

[15] Ibid, p.19

[16] "Muhammad Ali: The boxing icon's 10 best quotes", May Bulman, The Independent, 2016, https://www.independent.co.uk/news/people/muhammad-ali-quotes-dead-death-boxing-icon-float-like-butterfly-inspirational-a7065326.html

[17] Ibid, p.21

[18] "Swim, Bike, Run: Our Triathlon Story", Alistair Brownlee and Jonathan Brownlee, Penguin, 2014, p.10

[19] "No Limits: The Will to Succeed", Michael Phelps and Alan Abrahamson, Simon & Schuster UK, 2009, p.71

4. Coaches

[1] "Paula: My Story So Far", Paula Radcliffe, Simon & Schuster UK, 2005.

[2] Ibid, p.32

[3] Ibid, p.44

[4] Ibid, p.48

[5] Ibid, p.50

[6] "Paula Radcliffe", Wikipedia, accessed March 2018, https://en.wikipedia.org/wiki/Paula_Radcliffe

[7] "No Limits: The Will to Succeed", Michael Phelps and Alan Abrahamson, Simon & Schuster UK, 2009, p.19

[8] "Insight: The greatest Olympian and his coach", Julian Linden, Reuters, 2012,

https://www.reuters.com/article/us-oly-end-phelps/insight-the-greatest-olympian-and-his-coach-idUSBRE87B06N20120812

9 "Michael Phelps' Final Turn", Wayne Drehs, ESPN, 2016, http://www.espn.com/espn/feature/story/_/id/16425548/michael-phelps-prepares-life-2016-rio-olympics

10 "Michael Phelps", Wikipedia, accessed March 2018, https://en.wikipedia.org/wiki/Michael_Phelps

11 "The complicated relationship that molded Michael Phelps into the greatest", Pat Forde, Yahoo Sports, 2016, http://sports.yahoo.com/news/michael-phelps-bob-bowman-greatest-000000911.html

12 "No Limits: The Will to Succeed", Michael Phelps and Alan Abrahamson, Simon & Schuster UK, 2009, p.115

13 "Insight: The greatest Olympian and his coach", Julian Linden, Reuters, 2012, https://www.reuters.com/article/us-oly-end-phelps/insight-the-greatest-olympian-and-his-coach-idUSBRE87B06N20120812

14 "The Golden Rules: 10 Steps to World-Class Excellence in Your Life and Work", Bob Bowman, St. Martin's Press, 2016.

15 Ibid, p.17 – 18.

16 "Coach Effectiveness Training: A Cognitive-Behavioral Approach to Enhancing Relationship Skills in Youth Sport Coaches", Ronald Smith, Frank Smoll and Bill Curtis, Journal of Sport Psychology, 1979, https://journals.humankinetics.com/doi/abs/10.1123/jsp.1.1.59

17 Effects of Enhancing Coach-Athlete Relationships on Youth Sport Attrition, Nancy Barnett, Frank Smoll and Ronald Smith, The Sport Psychologist, 1992.

18 "The coach-athlete partnership", Sophia Jowett, Loughborough University, 2005, https://www.researchgate.net/profile/Sophia_Jowett/publication/290265291_The_coach-athlete_partnership/links/56a9ee4208aeaeb4cefa4b8c.pdf

19 "Black and White: The Way I See It", Richard Williams, Atria Books, 2014.

5. Parents

1 "My Life: Queen of the Court", Serena Williams, Simon & Schuster UK, 2010, p.11

[2] "Black and White: The Way I See It", Richard Williams, Atria Books, 2014.

[3] Ibid, p. 131 - 132

[4] Ibid, p. 132- 133

[5] Ibid, p.142

[6] Ibid, p.161

[7] Ibid, p. 161-2

[8] Ibid, p.190

[9] "World Cup 2014: Futsal - the game behind Brazil's superstars", Ben Smith, BBC Sport, 2014, accessed January 2018, http://www.bbc.co.uk/sport/football/27980859

[10] "The football greats forged by futsal", FIFA.com, 2012, accessed January 2018, http://www.fifa.com/futsalworldcup/news/y=2012/m=10/news=the-football-greats-forged-futsal-1798909.html

[11] "My Life: Queen of the Court, Serena Williams, Simon & Schuster UK, 2010.

[12] Ibid, p.29

[13] "Venus Williams", Wikipedia, accessed March 2018, https://en.wikipedia.org/wiki/Venus_Williams

[14] "Venus Williams", Wikipedia, accessed March 2018, https://en.wikipedia.org/wiki/Venus_Williams

[15] "Serena Williams", Wikipedia, accessed March 2018, https://en.wikipedia.org/wiki/Serena_Williams

[16] "Serena Williams Net Worth", TheRichest, accessed March 2018, https://www.therichest.com/celebnetworth/athletes/tennis/serena-williams-net-worth/

[17] "Venus Williams Net Worth", TheRichest, accessed March 2018, https://www.therichest.com/celebnetworth/athletes/tennis/venus-williams-net-worth/

[18] "Grit: The power of passion and perseverance" Angela Duckworth, Scribner Book Company, 2016

[19] "Faster Than Lightning: My Story", Usain Bolt, HarperSport, 2014, p.23

[20] "Usain Bolt's Parents: 5 Fast Facts You Need to Know", Tim Keeney, Heavy, 2016, accessed Jan 2018, https://heavy.com/sports/2016/08/usain-bolt-parents-father-mother-family-pictures-together-names-wellesley-jennifer-house-hometown-jamaica-bio/

[21] "Faster Than Lightning: My Story", Usain Bolt, HarperSport, 2014, p.17

[22] "Training a Tiger: A Father's Guide to Raising A Winner in Both Golf and Life", Earl Woods with Pete McDaniel, William Marrow, 1997.

[23] Ibid, p.4 - 5

[24] "The Secret History of Tiger Woods", Wright Thompson, ESPN, 2016, accessed January 2018, http://www.espn.com/espn/feature/story/_/id/15278522/how-tiger-woods-life-unraveled-years-father-earl-woods-death

6. Siblings

[1] "Jonny Brownlee helped over line by brother Alistair", John Chambers, 2016 [YouTube], accessed March 2018, https://www.youtube.com/watch?v=liCRrheKlOI

[2] "Alistair Brownlee gives up chance to win triathlon and helps brother over line", Guardian Sport, The Guardian, 2016, https://www.theguardian.com/sport/2016/sep/19/alistair-brownlee-jonny-world-triathlon-series

[3] "Swim, Bike, Run: Our Triathlon Story", Alistair Brownlee, Jonathan Brownlee, Penguin, 2014

[4] Ibid, p.1-2

[5] Ibid, p.71

[6] "Triathlon marred as Alistair Brownlee collapses in Hyde Park", Steve Skerry, MailOnline, 2010, accessed January 2018, http://www.dailymail.co.uk/sport/othersports/article-1297620/Triathlon-marred-Alistair-Brownlee-collapses-Hyde-Park.html

[7] "Interview: Olympic Gold Medallist - Alistair Brownlee MBE", Nick Butler, The Cambridge Student, 2013, https://www.tcs.cam.ac.uk/interviews/0027213-tcs-sport-exclusive-interview-olympic-gold-medallist-alistair-brownlee-mbe.html

[8] "Black and White: The Way I See It", Richard Williams, Atria Books, 2014.

[9] "My Life: Queen of the Court", Serena Williams, Simon & Schuster UK, 2010, p.43

[10] Ibid, p.44

[11] Ibid, p.43

[12] Ibid, p.59 - 60

[13] "Venus talks sister Serena's engagement amid first-round win in Australia", Sandra Harwitt, USA Today, 2017, http://www.usatoday.com/story/sports/tennis/2017/01/16/venus

-williams-serena-engagement-first-round-australian-open/96630416/

[14] "Pathways to the Podium", accessed March 2018, http://www.yorku.ca/podium/

[15] "Faster, higher, stronger... and younger? Birth order, sibling sport participation, and sport expertise development", Pathways to Podium Research Team, 2012, accessed March 2018, https://expertadvantage.wordpress.com/2012/06/19/siblings/

7.   School

[1] "Swim, Bike, Run: Our Triathlon Story", Alistair Brownlee, Jonathan Brownlee, Penguin, 2014, p.14

[2] Ibid, p.15

[3] Ibid, p.15

[4] "Sachin was a big-time bully!", Atul Ranade, accessed March 2018, http://m.rediff.com/cricket/2002/sep/03atul.htm

[5] "Playing It My Way: My Autobiography", Sachin Tendulkar, Hodder Paperbacks, 2015, p.15

[6] Ibid, p.17

[7] "Ramakant Achrekar's Top 5 students who made it big", Yedu Krishnan, sportskeeda, 2015, https://www.sportskeeda.com/slideshow/cricket-ramakant-achrekars-top-5-students-who-made-it-big

[8] "Sachin Tendulkar, Wikipedia, accessed March 2018, https://en.wikipedia.org/wiki/Sachin_Tendulkar

[9] Ibid, p.17

[10] Ibid, p.28

[11] "No Limits: The Will to Succeed", Michael Phelps and Alan Abrahamson, Simon & Schuster UK, 2009.

[12] Ibid, p.72

[13] "10 Reasons Why High School Sports Benefit Students", Grace Chen, 2018, accessed July 2018, https://www.publicschoolreview.com/blog/10-reasons-why-high-school-sports-benefit-students

8.   Sporting Bodies

[1] "The Bolt Supremacy: Inside Jamaica's Sprint Factory", Richard Moore, Yellow Jersey, 2015.

[2] "Nadia Comăneci", Wikipedia, accessed March 2018, https://en.wikipedia.org/wiki/Nadia_Comaneci

[3] "Letters to a Young Gymnast", Nadia Comăneci, Basic Books, 2011, p.11 - 12

[4] Ibid, p.11

[5] Ibid, p.17

[6] Ibid, p.18 - 19

[7] "Comaneci says childhood was not lost", Simon Evans, Reuters, 2008, accessed Jan 2018, https://in.reuters.com/article/idINIndia-34791620080802

[8]"The Karolyis' Tainted Glory", Jessica Winter, Slate, 2016, http://www.slate.com/articles/sports/fivering_circus/2016/08/martha_karolyi_and_her_husband_bela_were_great_coaches_they_als_o_allegedly.html

[9] Ibid

[10] Ibid

[11] "Countries in the world by population (2018)", Worldometers, http://www.worldometers.info/world-population/population-by-country/

[12] "Athletics in Jamaica", Wikipedia, accessed July 2018, https://en.wikipedia.org/wiki/Athletics_in_Jamaica

[13] "Faster Than Lightning: My Story", Usain Bolt, HarperSport, 2014, p.9 - 10

[14] Ibid, p.10

[15] "Inter-Secondary Schools Boys and Girls Championships", Wikipedia, accessed March 2018, https://en.wikipedia.org/wiki/Inter-Secondary_Schools_Boys_and_Girls_Championships

[17] "Faster Than Lightning: My Story", Usain Bolt, HarperSport, 2014, p.47-48

[18] "Historical Funding Figures", UKSport, accessed March 2018, http://www.uksport.gov.uk/our-work/investing-in-sport/historical-funding-figures

9. Networks

[1] "Lewis Hamilton: My Story", Lewis Hamilton, HarperSport, 2008, p.78

[2] Ibid, p.80

[3] "How Lewis Hamilton opened the eyes of McLaren's Ron Dennis", Alison Kervin, The Telegraph, 2008, https://www.telegraph.co.uk/sport/motorsport/formulaone/lewishamilton/3393413/How-Lewis-Hamilton-opened-the-eyes-of-McLarens-Ron-Dennis-Formula-One.html

[4] "Lewis Hamilton: My Story", Lewis Hamilton, HarperSport, 2008, p.46

[5] "How Lewis Hamilton opened the eyes of McLaren's Ron Dennis", Alison Kervin, The Telegraph, 2008, https://www.telegraph.co.uk/sport/motorsport/formulaone/lewishamilton/3393413/How-Lewis-Hamilton-opened-the-eyes-of-McLarens-Ron-Dennis-Formula-One.html

[6] "Training a Tiger: A Father's Guide to Raising A Winner in Both Golf and Life", Earl Woods and Pete McDaniel, William Marrow, 1997.

[7] Ibid, p.199

[8] "The rise of the triathlon holiday", Vanessa Barford, BBC Magazine, 2013, accessed January 2018, http://www.bbc.co.uk/news/magazine-23928730

[9] "Swim, Bike, Run: Our Triathlon Story", Alistair Brownlee, Jonathan Brownlee, Penguin, 2014, p.11 - 12

[10] Ibid, p.18

[11] Ibid, p.18

10. Practice

[1] "Outliers: The Story of Success", Malcolm Gladwell, Penguin, 2009, p.35

[2] "Bounce: The Myth of Talent and the Power of Practice", Matthew Syed, Fourth Estate, 2011.

[3] "The Sports Gene: Talent, Practice and the Truth about Success", David Epstein, Yellow Jersey, 2014.

[4] "Bounce: The Myth of Talent and the Power of Practice", Matthew Syed, Fourth Estate, 2011.

[5] "The Sports Gene: Talent, Practice and the Truth about Success", David Epstein, Yellow Jersey, 2014.

[6] "Peak: Secrets from the New Science of Expertise", Anders Ericsson and Robert Pool, Bodley Head, 2016, p.109.

[7] Ibid, p.99

[8] Ibid, p.99

[9] Ibid, p.100

[10] Ibid, p.100

[11] "An Overview and Critique of the '10,000 hours rule' and 'Theory of Deliberate Practise'", J North, Leeds Met University, 2012, http://eprints.leedsbeckett.ac.uk/78/1/North%2C%20J%20-%20An%20Overview%20and%20Critique%20of%20TDP%20and%2010%2C000%20Hours%20Rule%20-%20Report%20-%20Final.pdf

[12] "Playing It My Way: My Autobiography", Sachin Tendulkar, Hodder Paperbacks, 2015, p.15

[13] "Cricket: A bat, a ball, and a million dreams", Richard Williams, The Independent, 1993, accessed July 2018,
https://www.independent.co.uk/sport/cricket-a-bat-a-ball-and-a-million-dreams-the-england-cricket-teams-winter-tour-has-brought-home-the-1474315.html

[14] "Ramakant Achrekar", Wikipedia, accessed March 2018,
https://en.wikipedia.org/wiki/Ramakant_Achrekar

[15] "We have the talent, our problem is attitude!" Bhishan Mansukani, Rediff on the Net, 1998, accessed March 2018,
http://www.rediff.com/sports/1998/jul/20a.htm

[16] "No Limits: The Will to Succeed", Michael Phelps and Alan Abrahamson, Simon & Schuster UK, 2009.

[17] Ibid, p. 68.

[18] Ibid, p.108

[19] Ibid, p.108

[20] Ibid, p.109

[21] "When Michael Phelps Was Just a Teenager | Before They Were Superstars", Olympics, 2017 [YouTube], accessed March 2018,
https://www.youtube.com/watch?v=jm6qcEDVz9g&t=127s

[22] "Michael Phelps", Wikipedia, accessed March 2018,
https://en.wikipedia.org/wiki/Michael_Phelps

[23] "Letters to a Young Gymnast", Nadia Comăneci, Basic Books, 2011.

[24] "Michael Phelps", Wikipedia, accessed March 2018,
https://en.wikipedia.org/wiki/Michael_Phelps

[25] "All-time Olympic Games medal table", Wikipedia,
https://en.wikipedia.org/wiki/All-time_Olympic_Games_medal_table

[26] "The Golden Rules: Finding World-Class Excellence in Your Life and Work", Bob Bowman, St Martin's Press, 2016.

[27] "Peak: Secrets from the New Science of Expertise", Anders Ericcson and Robert Pool, Bodley Head, 2016, p.99

11. The History of Practice

[1] "Are athletes really getting faster, better, stronger?", David Epstein, TED talk, 2014,
https://www.ted.com/talks/david_epstein_are_athletes_really_getting_faster_better_stronger

[2] "Interview Sir Roger Bannister", Donald McRae, The Guardian, 2004, accessed March 2018,
https://www.theguardian.com/sport/2004/apr/26/athletics

[3] "Mile Run World Record Progression", Wikipedia, accessed March 2018,
https://en.wikipedia.org/wiki/Mile_run_world_record_progression

[4] First Four Minute Mile -HQ (Roger Bannister) – AthletixStuffChannel, 2012, [YouTube]
https://www.youtube.com/watch?v=wTXoTnp_5sI

[5] "Mile Run World Record Progression", Wikipedia, accessed March 2018,
https://en.wikipedia.org/wiki/Mile_run_world_record_progression

[6] "Twin Tracks: The Autobiography", Roger Bannister, The Robson Press, 2015, p.38-9.

[7] "Twin Tracks: The Autobiography", Roger Bannister, The Robson Press, 2015, p.101-2.

[8] "Interview Sir Roger Bannister", The Guardian, 2004,
https://www.theguardian.com/sport/2004/apr/26/athletics

[9] "Running My Life – The Autobiography", Seb Coe, Hodder & Stoughton, 2012, p.104.

[10] Ibid, p.31

[11] Ibid, p.41

[12] "Sebastian Coe", Wikipedia, accessed March 2018,
https://en.wikipedia.org/wiki/Sebastian_Coe

[13] "Sebastian Coe", Wikipedia, accessed March 2018,
https://en.wikipedia.org/wiki/Sebastian_Coe

[14] "Julius Yego", Wikipedia, accessed March 2018,
https://en.wikipedia.org/wiki/Julius_Yego

[15] "GoPro: Julius Yego – The YouTube Man", GoPro, 2016, [YouTube], https://www.youtube.com/watch?v=lO1fzo1aCHU

[16] "The Short Game", Josh Greenaum, 2013, Netflix,
https://www.netflix.com/title/70290567

12. Luck

[1] "Ben Collett", Wikipedia, accessed March 2018,
https://en.wikipedia.org/wiki/Ben_Collett

[2] "Neville - Collett was top-level", Andy Murray, Manchester Evening News, 2010, accessed April 2018,

https://www.manchestereveningnews.co.uk/news/greater-manchester-news/neville--collett-was-top-level-959379

[3] "Manchester United F.C. Reserves and Academy", Wikipedia, accessed March 2018, https://en.wikipedia.org/wiki/Manchester United F.C. Reserves an d Academy#Players of the Year

[4] "Neville - Collett was top-level", Andy Murray, Manchester Evening News, 2010, accessed April 2018, https://www.manchestereveningnews.co.uk/news/greater-manchester-news/neville--collett-was-top-level-959379

[5] "Neville - Collett was top-level", Andy Murray, Manchester Evening News, 2010, accessed April 2018, https://www.manchestereveningnews.co.uk/news/greater-manchester-news/neville--collett-was-top-level-959379

[6] "The £4.3million football career that never was", Mark Hughes, The Independent, 2008, accessed April 2018, https://www.independent.co.uk/news/uk/home-news/the-16343million-football-career-that-never-was-891508.html

[7] "Neville - Collett was top-level", Andy Murray, Manchester Evening News, 2010, accessed April 2018, https://www.manchestereveningnews.co.uk/news/greater-manchester-news/neville--collett-was-top-level-959379

[8] "The £4.3million football career that never was", Mark Hughes, The Independent, 2008, https://www.independent.co.uk/news/uk/home-news/the-16343million-football-career-that-never-was-891508.html

[9] "Football, running and rugby revealed to carry the greatest risk of injury in new Benenden research", 2016, Benenden Healthcare, accessed August 2018, https://www.benenden.co.uk/newsroom/football-running-and-rugby-revealed-to-carry-the-greatest-risk-of-injury/

[10] "No Limits: The Will to Succeed", Michael Phelps and Alan Abrahamson, Simon & Schuster UK, 2009, p.65.

[11] "The Golden Rules: 10 Steps to World-Class Excellence in Your Life and Work", Bob Bowman, St. Martin's Press, 2016, p.263

[12] "Michael Phelps' Final Turn, Wayne Drehs, ESPN Magazine, 2016,http://www.espn.com/espn/feature/story/ /id/16425548/michael-phelps-prepares-life-2016-rio-olympics

[13] "Outliers: The Story of Success", Malcolm Gladwell, Penguin, 2009.

[14] "Playing It My Way: My Autobiography", Sachin Tendulkar, Hodder Paperbacks, 2015, p.15

13. Genetics

[1] "Lionel Messi: Magic in his feet", John Carlin, The Independent, 2010, accessed April 2018,
https://www.independent.co.uk/news/people/profiles/lionel-messi-magic-in-his-feet-1928768.html

[2] "Lionel Messi", Wikipedia, accessed March 2018,
https://en.wikipedia.org/wiki/Lionel_Messi

[3] "Lionel Messi: Magic in his feet", John Carlin, The Independent, 2010, accessed April 2018,
https://www.independent.co.uk/news/people/profiles/lionel-messi-magic-in-his-feet-1928768.html

[4] "Lionel Messi's improbable progression from struggling youngster to world super star", Guillem Balague, Telegraph, 2013, accessed April 2018,
https://www.telegraph.co.uk/sport/football/players/lionel-messi/10487181/Lionel-Messis-improbable-progression-from-struggling-youngster-to-world-super-star.html

[5] "Lionel Messi", Wikipedia, accessed March 2018,
https://en.wikipedia.org/wiki/Lionel_Messi

[6] "Lionel Messi", Wikipedia, accessed March 2018,
https://en.wikipedia.org/wiki/Lionel_Messi

[7] "How Golden Ball winner Lionel Messi overcame growth hormone deficiency to become the best in the world", Pavitra Sampath, The Health Site, 2014, accessed April 2018,
http://www.thehealthsite.com/news/how-golden-ball-winner-lionel-messi-overcame-growth-hormone-deficiency-to-become-the-best-in-the-world/

[8] "Lionel Messi's improbable progression from struggling youngster to world super star", Guillem Balague, Telegraph, 2013, accessed April 2018,
https://www.telegraph.co.uk/sport/football/players/lionel-messi/10487181/Lionel-Messis-improbable-progression-from-struggling-youngster-to-world-super-star.html

[9] "Does the lack of academy graduates in the Premier League simply reflect its growing quality?", Alex Keble, The Independent, 2015, accessed August 2018,

https://www.independent.co.uk/sport/football/premier-league/does-the-lack-of-academy-graduates-in-the-premier-league-simply-reflect-its-growing-quality-a6730551.html

[10] "Lionel Messi: how Argentinian teenager signed for Barcelona on a serviette", Sid Lowe, The Guardian, 2014, https://www.theguardian.com/football/blog/2014/oct/15/lionel-messi-barcelona-decade

[11] "Lionel Messi: how Argentinian teenager signed for Barcelona on a serviette", Sid Lowe, The Guardian, 2014, https://www.theguardian.com/football/blog/2014/oct/15/lionel-messi-barcelona-decade

[12] "Lionel Messi: how Argentinian teenager signed for Barcelona on a serviette", Sid Lowe, The Guardian, 2014, https://www.theguardian.com/football/blog/2014/oct/15/lionel-messi-barcelona-decade

[13] "Lionel Messi's improbable progression from struggling youngster to world super star", Guillem Balague, Telegraph, 2013, https://www.telegraph.co.uk/sport/football/players/lionel-messi/10487181/Lionel-Messis-improbable-progression-from-struggling-youngster-to-world-super-star.html

[14] "Messi destroyed Barcelona team-mates at 16 – Giuly", Stefan Coerts, Goal.com, http://www.goal.com/en-gb/news/3277/la-liga/2016/09/14/27518542/messi-destroyed-barcelona-team-mates-at-16-giuly

[15] "Lionel Messi", Wikipedia, accessed March 2018, https://en.wikipedia.org/wiki/Lionel_Messi

[16] "Tactical Analysis Of The Barcelona Tiki Taka Playing Style", Espen, Passion4FM, 2015, https://www.passion4fm.com/tactical-analysis-of-the-barcelona-tiki-taka-playing-style/

[17] "Ronaldo 7", realmadrid.com, https://www.realmadrid.com/en/football/squad/cristiano-ronaldo-dos-santos

[18] "Football talent spotting: Are clubs getting it wrong with kids?", Alistair Magowan, BBC Sport, 2015, accessed August 2018, https://www.bbc.co.uk/sport/football/35054310

[19] "Olympic Archery: By The Numbers", World Archery, https://worldarchery.org/news/142050/olympic-archery-numbers

[20] "How much of human height is genetic and how much is due to nutrition?", Dr. Chao-Qiang Lai, Scientific American,

https://www.scientificamerican.com/article/how-much-of-human-height/

[21] "Is athletic performance determined by genetics?", Genetics Home Reference, US National History of Medicine, accessed August 2018, https://ghr.nlm.nih.gov/primer/traits/athleticperformance

[22] "The Wilson Effect: The Increase in Heritability of IQ With Age", Bouchard, Twin Research and Human Genetics, 2013, accessed August 2018, https://www.gwern.net/docs/iq/2013-bouchard.pdf

[23] "Heritability estimates of the Big Five personality traits based on common genetic variants", Power and Pleuss, Translational Psychiatry, 2015, accessed March 2018, https://www.nature.com/articles/tp201596

[24] "Helen Glover's Olympic gold first for UK talent scheme", Jenny Minard, BBC News, 2012, accessed April 2018, http://www.bbc.co.uk/news/uk-19081992

[25] "Sporting Giants", Wikipedia, accessed March 2018, https://en.wikipedia.org/wiki/Sporting_Giants

[26] "Sporting Giants", Wikipedia, accessed March 2018, https://en.wikipedia.org/wiki/Sporting_Giants

[27] "Olympic gold rower Helen Glover's 'phenomenal talent'", BBC News, 2012, http://www.bbc.co.uk/news/uk-england-cornwall-19076903

[28] "Helen Glover's Olympic gold first for UK talent scheme", Jenny Minard, BBC News, 2012, http://www.bbc.co.uk/news/uk-19081992

[29] "Helen Glover", Wikipedia, accessed March 2018, https://en.wikipedia.org/wiki/Helen_Glover_(rower)

14. The Nearly Ones

[1] "Our Mission", accessed April 2018, http://www.heisman.com/heisman-trust/

[2] "Heisman Trophy", Wikipedia, accessed March 2018, https://en.wikipedia.org/wiki/Heisman_Trophy

[3] "Terry Baker", Wikipedia, accessed March 2018, https://en.wikipedia.org/wiki/Terry_Baker

[4] "Sportsman of the Year: Terry Baker", Alfred Wright, Sports Illustrated, 1963, https://www.si.com/vault/1963/01/07/598703/sportsman-of-the-year-terry-baker

[5] "Sports Illustrated Sportsperson of the Year", Wikipedia, accessed March 2018,

https://en.wikipedia.org/wiki/Sports_Illustrated_Sportsperson_of_th
e_Year

[6] "Sportsman of the Year: Terry Baker", Alfred Wright, Sports Illustrated, 1963, accessed March 2018, https://www.si.com/vault/1963/01/07/598703/sportsman-of-the-year-terry-baker

[7] Ibid

[8] "NW #1 rate QB Terry Baker's 99 yard record Liberty Bowl Run", 2009, YouTube [03:23], accessed March 2018, https://www.youtube.com/watch?v=ZaCi9JO0cVE

[9] Pac-12 Living Legend: Oregon State's Terry Baker, YouTube, 2015, https://www.youtube.com/watch?v=ZxeGsgLVXkU

[10] "Terry Baker", Wikipedia, accessed March 2018, https://en.wikipedia.org/wiki/Terry_Baker

[11] Pac-12 Living Legend: Oregon State's Terry Baker, YouTube, 2015, https://www.youtube.com/watch?v=ZxeGsgLVXkU

[12] Sportsman of the Year: Terry Baker", Alfred Wright, Sports Illustrated, 1963, accessed March 2018, https://www.si.com/vault/1963/01/07/598703/sportsman-of-the-year-terry-baker

[13] "Two Big Surprises: Longshot Makes It, a Sureshot Doesn't : TERRY BAKER : He Seemed to Have It All and the Rams Went for It", Rich Roberts, LA Times, 1987, http://articles.latimes.com/1987-04-26/sports/sp-1348_1_college-football-awards

[14] "Terry Baker: A Different Success", Beau Riffenburgh, Coffin Corner, 1987, accessed March 2018, p.2, http://profootballresearchers.com/archives/Website_Files/Coffin_C orner/09-07-308.pdf

[15] "Terry Baker: A Different Success", Beau Riffenburgh, Coffin Corner, 1987, accessed March 2018, p.2, http://profootballresearchers.com/archives/Website_Files/Coffin_C orner/09-07-308.pdf

[16] "Two Big Surprises: Longshot Makes It, a Sureshot Doesn't : TERRY BAKER : He Seemed to Have It All and the Rams Went for It", Rich Roberts, LA Times, 1987, http://articles.latimes.com/1987-04-26/sports/sp-1348_1_college-football-awards

[17] "Terry Baker", NFL.com, http://www.nfl.com/player/terrybaker/2508896/careerstats

[18]"Tim Tebow's unusual education", Valerie Strauss, Washington Post, 2012, accessed March 2018,
https://www.washingtonpost.com/blogs/answer-sheet/post/tim-tebows-unusual-education/2012/01/10/gIQAxhffyP_blog.html?utm_term=.ef9140eb3c11

[19] Ibid

[20] Ibid

[21] "Tim Tebow", Wikipedia, accessed March 2018,
https://en.wikipedia.org/wiki/Tim_Tebow

[22] "Tim Tebow", Wikipedia, accessed March 2018,
https://en.wikipedia.org/wiki/Tim_Tebow

[23] "Youth football participation increases in 2015; teen involvement down, data shows", Tom Farrey, ESPN, 2016,
http://www.espn.com/espn/otl/story/_/id/15210245/slight-one-year-increase-number-youth-playing-football-data-shows

[24] "Football", NCAA Research, NCAA.org,
http://www.ncaa.org/about/resources/research/football

[25] "The NFL's Highest-Paid Players 2016", Kurt Badenhausen, Forbes, 2016,
https://www.forbes.com/sites/kurtbadenhausen/2016/09/14/the-nfls-highest-paid-players-2016/#3e81f155713a

Printed in Great Britain
by Amazon